P9-DFE-894

THEATRICAL DANCING IN AMERICA

THEATRICAL DANCING IN AMERICA

The Development of the Ballet from 1900

Second Edition, Revised

WINTHROP PALMER

SOUTH BRUNSWICK AND NEW YORK: A. S. Barnes and Company
LONDON: Thomas Yoseloff Ltd

792.809
P182t

LIBRARY
ATLANTIC CHRISTIAN COLLEGE
WILSON, N. C.

New Material © 1978 by A. S. Barnes and Co., Inc.
Library of Congress Catalog Card Number: 76-58582

A. S. Barnes and Co., Inc.
Cranbury, New Jersey 08512

Thomas Yoseloff Ltd
Magdalen House
136–148 Tooley Street
London SE1 2TT, England

TO
AMERICAN THEATRICAL DANCERS

ISBN 0-498-02108-4
Printed in the United States of America

CONTENTS

7

AUG 0 5 1983

Gen. 3.95

83— 0828

PREFACE

Ballet, a form of dance and pantomime, expresses the spirit of a people in terms of movement and gesture. It reveals character, aspirations, ideals, fears and frenzy—also, faith.

Ballet is a plastic form of poetry. It reminds us that life is *not* a photograph, nor a newspaper, nor an unseen oracle, but is the sensation of feeling. Ballet, an expression in dance and pantomime, is a great art to which this book is soberly dedicated.

INTRODUCTION

ON VAUDEVILLE

Vaudeville is a French word. Its origin is said to be either *voix de ville*, street songs, or *chansons de vaux de vire*, popular topical or satirical drinking songs composed in the Calvados, Normandy, by a fifteenth-century literary society whose most famous member was the poet Olivier Basselin. The *vaux de vire* songs were written in couplets and were sung to popular tunes. In 1674 the word *vaudeville* was used by the grammarian-poet Boileau to describe ballads of this kind.

The word *vaudeville* entered the official theatre vocabulary in eighteenth-century France when professional actors and strolling players took pantomime, song, and dance to the streets and the country fairs to get around the dramatic monopoly of the state theatre, the Comédie Française, sole licensee of legitimate drama.

In the United States, "variety entertainment" was supported and encouraged from the earliest times by the colonies and the new states. Scattered settlements were ready and waiting for the arrival of strolling acrobats, ballad singers, and story-tellers. But the word *vaudeville* was not used to describe this kind of entertainment until after the Civil War.

In the 1850s and 60s performances at "concert saloons," nicknamed "dumps and slabs" by their male patrons, replaced the minstrel show. Dump-and-slab programs catered to lower-class taste. They were always vulgar and sometimes obscene, as were the cow-barn performances of "what happened back of the haystack" with comment by sledgehammer comics.

In the eighties, every hustling new town in America had a *variety hall*, the club or social center of the red-light district. On Saturday night, miners, railroad workers, farmers, cowboys,

11

and ranchers fought bare handed in the back of the hall. Prostitutes ("genuine sluts") wore elaborate, French-style get-ups and used elegant perfume. The comics who entertained this audience earned fifteen dollars a week. They learned how to handle a brawl a night.

"The backbone of American vaudeville," writes Douglas Gilbert, "was low comedy."*

It was also the backbone of many scenes from the classic theatre of Aristophanes, Plautus, Terence, Shakespeare, and Molière. A theatre child, low comedy must learn many disciplines —precision, polish, timing, and many techniques, such as juggling, mime, ballad singing, dancing, and acrobatics. The techniques were not an end in themselves. They were a preparation for putting across low comedy's message. That message was (and is) a satirical view of the life of the times in popular language, gesture, and movement.

Cow-barn, beer-hall, and variety entertainment went out of favor as social life in American towns settled down. New audiences were more "responsive" than the old stag crowd, and acts improved. So did the salaries of clog dancers, aerial teams, female impersonators, dialect comedians, trios, quartets, pantomimists, and monologists. "Refined vaudeville" as opposed to "variety" was introduced to the family trade in America by Tony Pastor. Antonio Pastor (1837–1908) was born in New York City of theatre people. His father played the violin at Mitchell's Opera House, his older brothers were aerialists and circus riders.

At six Tony Pastor was singing comedy duets at temperance meetings. At nine he sang in blackface at Barnum's Museum. He was hired by a touring menagerie as clown, ballad singer, low comedian, and general performer when he was ten. At fifteen he was circus ringmaster and singing clown. He was twenty-eight when he opened his own music hall on the Bowery. He called it Tony Pastor's Opera House, and he packed them in with his historical topical songs about events in the Civil War. He sang history into the theatre.

To sing (or dance) American history into the theatre, who did that after Tony Pastor? George M. Cohan did during the First World War. Gene Kelly (*Pal Joey*) and Harold Rome (*Pins and Needles*) in the Depression years. Jerome Robbins danced and choreographed the city after World War II, and Alvin Ailey

* Douglas Gilbert, *History of American Vaudeville* (Dover, 1940).

danced and choreographed the civil rights revolution of the 1950s and 60s.

His fans gave Tony Pastor the title "Father of American Vaudeville" (pronounced *vodvil*), and they followed him from the Opera House on the Bowery to the Music Hall on 14th Street and in '88 to the one on Union Square.

What kind of a bill "packed them in" at Tony Pastor's, men, women, young people, and the family trade? A very diversified bill. Something for everyone, the basic requirement of popular entertainment.

A song-and-dance team opened the bill. They warmed up the house. (Television, pinch-hitting for vaudeville, has had to skip dance teams and dance in general. Cameras and human bodies in the movements of dance just don't get together!) After the dance team came a singer, then a comedy sketch, and then a monologist with a specialty, either juggling or rope-swinging. (Will Rogers and W. C. Fields would make this act famous in the twenties, in Florenz Ziegfeld's Follies at the New Amsterdam Theatre in New York.)

Every bill at Tony Pastor's had a dramatic skit (*The Valiant* was sure-fire), followed by a musical act from the legitimate theatre, a headliner like Eva Tanguay, the I-Don't-Care girl, and an acrobatic troupe to wind things up.

FROM BAGGY PANTS AND FRIGHT WIGS
TO ANNA PAVLOWA

Veteran comics had no use for the straight, clean, variety show. The profession's Old Guard accused Tony Pastor of castrating vaudeville to accommodate a Sunday School picnic, and they prophesied that the public would not put up with this.

They were mistaken. There were fewer and fewer laughs for slapstick shoes and dialect jokes. Tony Pastor's style of vaudeville was introduced to the nation by the entrepreneurs Martin Beck (the Orpheum circuit), Benjamin Franklin Keith, and Edward Franklin Albee (the Keith-Albee circuit). Beck controlled vaudeville houses from Chicago to California and the Palace Theatre in New York City. Keith-Albee's four hundred theatres were in the East and Midwest.

The visiting dance team from Russia invited by Otto Kahn to perform at the Metropolitan Opera House in 1910 had everything going for it when it hit the road after the instant success in Léo Délibes's three-act ballet *Coppelia* at the Metropolitan. Anna Pavlowa and her partners (she changed them frequently) danced in vaudeville houses in New York and across the country from 1912 to 1925, and a fairy story came true before the eyes of enchanted American audiences. They saw "a perfect dancer's body —strong and slim legs, long and lovely arms, an arching neck, exquisitely poised hands, a finely modeled torso—and a carefully schooled technique that made the difficult appear easy."* The fairy story became a legend that is fresh and alive today, the indispensable image of beauty and strength and grace.

Many other stars met the American public in vaudeville houses: Sarah Bernhardt, Yvette Guilbert, Maurice Chevalier. Straight, clean variety did not die of refinement. Some of it was taken over by the owners and operators of moving-picture cameras, recording equipment, and television. Some of it moved to the New Amsterdam Theatre, on 42nd Street, a few doors west of Broadway where Florenz Ziegfeld showed off a chorus line of beauties in an American version of the Folies Bérgère. After 1932 it turned up in musical comedy in the person of Gene Kelly (*Pal Joey*), in the comics Bert Lahr and Ed Wynne, and in such dance teams as Fred and Adele Astaire, also in the ballads and skits of *Pins and Needles,* a mock opera by Harold Rome.

Pins and Needles was produced by the International Ladies Garment Workers Union in the Labor Stage Theatre, West 39th Street, in 1937. It moved to Broadway and ran two years. Its hit songs (sung by Union members) "Sunday in the Park" and "Sing Me a Song of Social Significance" were the sharpest comment made by popular theatre on the social, economic, and political trends of the thirties.

In 1939, along came another Russian ballerina. Alicia Markova was introduced to America by Lucia Chase's Ballet Theatre. Markova danced in a now bull-dozed music hall once the splendid annex, two blocks south of Radio City Music Hall on Sixth Avenue.

* * * * *

From Tony Pastor's New Union Song Book—*1864*

THAT SOUTHERN WAGON

* Walter Terry, *The Dance in America* (Harper and Row, 1971).

(as sung by Tony Pastor)
(air—"Wait for the Wagon")

Jeff Davis built a wagon, and on it put his name,
And Beauregard was driver of Secession's ugly frame,
The horse he would get hungry, as most of horses do,
They had to keep the collar tight, to keep from pulling through.

Chorus: Bully for the wagon,
The new Secession wagon;
Oh, Beaury hold the nag in,
While you all take a ride.

The axles wanted greasing—the body wasn't wide;
North Carolina jumped into it, Mississippi by her side,
Virginia took a cushioned seat, and Louisiana next,
South Carolina got to "scrouging," and Florida got vexed.

They asked Kentucky to take a ride, she said "the horse was blind,"
She shook her head at seeing Tennessee jump on behind;
But Jeff assured her "all was right," the wagon it was new,
Missouri winked at Beauregard, and said "it wouldn't do."

Old Scott brought out *his* wagon—one that had run for years;
They caught old Union, hitched him up, and greased the running
gears.
Said Scott, "McClellan, you're the boy I want to fill my place,
So take the reins, and get the folks, and give Secesh a race."

New York and Pennsylvania, with a host of Yankee boys,
Got up into the wagon, and they called for Illinois;
And old Ohio, she jumped in, Missouri tried her luck,
And Indiana threw her arms around good old Kentuck.

Old Union threw his head back—he traveled rather slow
Until they reached Manassas—they hallooed "let him go";
Their cheers for Union made him put new mettle in his heel
He run into "Secession"—tore the spoke out of a wheel.

They took the broken wagon back, and put in all new spokes;
Secesh went down towards Kentuck, to tell it to the folks.
Old Union started after, and he made the welkin ring
When he ran into Secession at a little place—Mill Spring.

Secesh got scared and run away—the like was never seen;
Old Union threw his head back, and sailed through Bowling
Green,
Secesh ran to Cumberland and couldn't get across—
He broke the reins that guided him, and trusted to his hoss.

Old Union got his "dander up," and passed him "under way,"
He run into Fort Donelson, but didn't go to stay.
Tennessee fell out the wagon, and the balance of them cried,
And asked McClellan, as he passed, "Say, Mister, let us ride."

They went from there to Nashville, and there they'll change the
    scenes,
They'll grease the axle, turn old Union's head towards New
    Orleans;
They'll stop at Memphis, feed the hoss, and then they'll let him
    go,
To drag Secesh's rotten frame to the Gulf of Mexico.

Now Buckner he's gone up the spout, and Floyd has seen the sights,
And all the boys that went away with Buckner for their "rights"
Ah, boys, you've seen the elephant—I hope it won't be long
Till you'll be singing out with joy, "The Union, right or wrong."

From Tony Pastor's Comic Irish Songster—*1864*

THE FIFTH AVENUE BELLE

by Tony Pastor
(tune—"A Sentimental Strain")

There is none but a fool
That will wed on a sud – du – en,
Or take a fine belle
That cannot make a pud – du – en.
If he gets such a wife,
Then what would a man gain, oh,
But a dam – su – el that plays
On a forty pi – ay – no?

Some ladies than peacocks
Are twenty-five times prouderer;
Some ladies than thun – du – er
Are twenty-seven times louderer:
But I'll have a wife
That's obliging and ci – vu – el
And your Fifth Avenuedle belles
They may go to the divuel.

PART I

THE AMERICAN REVOLUTION

CHAPTER I

ISADORA DUNCAN

HER PRINCIPLES AND PERSONALITY

It has been said that Isadora Duncan was not a dancer because she refused to accept the contemporary forms of ballet and athletic dancing. But this is like saying Walt Whitman was not a poet because he did not write sonnets.

To my way of thinking, it seems important to analyze and classify Isadora Duncan's work as a dancer and creator of ballets as well as to recognize at the outset that she rebelled against the society of her time—a society which was a caste, in the United States, and to a certain extent, in Europe. A caste that ruled by the religion of education, with the priesthood of professors; it condemned as heathen and barbarian the healthy enjoyment of the senses, and exalted the functions of the intellect.

It seems necessary to underline and emphasize the fact that because Isadora Duncan pronounced: "The dance is not a diversion but a religion—the religion of beauty," does not mean that the dance before her time and the dance of her time, which she despised, was not also a religion. It seems important to observe that the dance she despised and scorned and which still exists, is the dance which makes a religion of diversion.

Did the choreographers of the ballet Isadora Duncan disliked because "it constrains people to adopt unnatural attitudes and cramps the free expressions of their emotions" deserve her scorn?

These choreographers were indicating the state of being of a people—the rule of a caste dedicated to certain ideas and principles, governed by the philosophy of materialism. It is assuredly

17

right and proper to disagree with the kind of philosophy, ideas and principles current or proposed. But should the category of the idea affect the judgment of the form of expression used to manifest that idea? Was Isadora Duncan honestly concerned with the principle of Dancing as an art form or as a personal expression of an individual emotion?

If the latter, she was not a classical, she was a romantic dancer.

Isadora Duncan was a challenge to the Puritan, the Cavalier and the Victorian alike. A challenge as the creator of a dance that demanded an immediate surrender on the part of the spectator to beauty in human form; that charged Puritans, Cavaliers and Victorians with class worship of wealth and power and social position, with the exaltation of gold and material possessions above all things, natural and spiritual. To her mind the symbols of Puritan, Cavalier and Victorian worship were fine clothes and ornaments that concealed or disguised misshapen, ugly bodies; they seemed to Isadora Duncan a tragic evidence of moral decay, of physical debauch and of a lethargic or lost spirit.

All the dancing of Isadora Duncan and her pupils was dedicated to a return to the original strength, grace, and natural movements of woman's body. "It is not only a question of true art, it is a question of race, of the development of the female sex to beauty and health. The dancing school of the future is to develop and to show the ideal form of woman."

Like Jean Jacques Rousseau, Isadora Duncan was the ferment that raised a revolution. When she gave her first performances, barefoot, in Greek costume with nothing but a plain blue curtain for scenery, she shocked an audience accustomed either to classic Italian ballet, with the dancer on toe in a filmy tu-tu, or to such popular style dance as Irene and Vernon Castle's mincing "Walk," Paderewski's "Minuet" and Pavlowa's "Gavotte."

These latter dances were the stylish forms taught in New York, Chicago, Philadelphia, San Francisco and Boston, and imitated by those who lived in smaller, less fashionable cities. But after 1908 and Isadora Duncan's memorable tour, the Castle Walk and the Minuet and the Gavotte and the finicky toe ballet appeared in a new and smaller dimension; these dances now appeared as belonging in the category of *genre,* which is the symbol of the manners of a class, not of the culture of a nation or a people.

"For the gymnast, the movement and culture of the body are an end in themselves. For the dancer they are the means of expression of the sentiments and thoughts of the soul."

This is not the statement of a Classicist. According to these remarks it would seem Isadora Duncan was not content with Beauty for its own sake, that her practices belied her principles.

Did she love her own body rather than the ideal of a beautiful form? The contemplation of a beautiful body in motion did not seem sufficient in her estimation. She demanded that the sensuous and the sensual be acknowledged to have a symbolic identification with the spiritual.

It is not difficult to understand why her attempt to make the Greek Chorus and the ancient tragic dance live again did not succeed. Since the essence of tragedy is the struggle between man's animal nature and his spiritual nature, any dance founded on the principle that these two natures did not conflict and that they were reconcilable without the anguish of sacrifice, had no drama. Such a dance could only be pictorial and, ultimately, hopelessly prosaic—glorious hocus-pocus or a noble self-delusion, nothing more. What saved Isadora's dance from becoming mere rhetorical posturing was the brilliant splendor of her melodic movement, an intuitive expression of the rhythm of timeless natural forces.

But other than as a social revolutionary, a pioneer in the theatre arts and in the character of an eloquent and beautiful solo dancer, Isadora Duncan did not accomplish great work. The individual transcended the accomplishment. For all her inspired worship of Beauty and Nature, the force of her own personality was not disciplined into any permanent form.

Who could revive a work of Isadora Duncan's today? But this is not said to belittle a great artist. Duncan may have personified her own emotion in the gestures she imitated from Greek vases; she admittedly did. But although she did not express the emotion of the American people in a dance idiom, she made it possible for others to do so. In her tunic and sandals she made a place for herself in the salons of Newport, the drawing rooms of London, and in competition with the "divertissement" of the Paris stage, because she had the courage and ability to accept costumes, lighting effects, and stage device as substitutes for the communication between a dancer and an audience, and because she insisted that drama came to be only through the physical medium of the body as an instrument of emotional and spiritual exchange between actor and audience.

ISADORA DUNCAN "ON STAGE" IN THE UNITED STATES

The young girl who taught dancing to children of rich families in San Francisco by the "new method" of interpreting poems by movement and gesture, came to New York in 1897 to join the Augustin Daly Company in a pantomime starring Jane May, famous pantomimist "from Paris."

Jane May acted "Pierrot," and Isadora Duncan in "a Directoire costume of blue silk, a blonde wig and a big straw hat" made love to Pierrot. Alas for the revolution of art she had come to give the world! The pantomime was a failure and closed after three weeks in New York and a three months' road tour of one-night stands.

Jane May went back to Paris and Isadora accepted Daly's offer of a dance part in his production of *A Midsummer Night's Dream*. Although interested in expressing human emotion and not fairy fancy, Isadora danced the Scherzo of Mendelssohn and made a hit. But Daly was displeased. "It is unheard of to have a dance number in a Shakespearean play. This isn't a music hall," Daly roared; and thereafter the lights were turned off when Isadora Duncan danced in *A Midsummer Night's Dream*.

But unhappy though she was, Isadora stayed on in Daly's "Shakespearean Company" for two years. She danced at the wedding of Miranda and Ferdinand in *The Tempest*, and as a gypsy in *Much Ado About Nothing*.

When the Shakespearean Company disbanded in 1899, Daly put Duncan in his production of *The Geisha*, but she balked at a singing role and resigned.

Her next performance was a concert with Ethelbert Nevin in the small Music Room of Carnegie Hall, where she danced *Narcissus, Ophelia, The Water Nymph* and *Spring*, with the composer at the piano. The concert was a great success and was followed by several others that led to engagements in New York drawing rooms, but no impresario could be found who would book the performance; and after a summer of dancing at Mrs. Astor's villa in Newport and a winter of teaching dancing classes at the Windsor Hotel in New York, Isadora embarked for London in a cattle boat to try to win an audience less cold than Augustin Daly, "the Smart Set at Newport, and the New York Four Hundred."

Isadora Duncan did not return to the United States until 1908. For eight years she worked in Europe—in London, Paris, Berlin, Leipsig, Munich, Vienna, Budapest, Florence, Venice, Athens, Bayreuth, St. Petersburg, Moscow, Kiev. Everywhere she was befriended by painters, poets and intellectuals. Drawing rooms were the scenes of her success; she was the rage of artistic and literary aides, but "theatre managers remained unmoved." A repertoire that had begun in London with interpretations of Ethelbert Nevin grew as Isadora studied the poetry, music, art and architecture of England, France, Germany, Italy, Greece and Russia.

After many months of seeking "the central spring of all movement, the crater of motor power, the unity from which all diversities of movements are born," she discovered the theory on which she founded her school.

Contrary to the teaching of the ballet master who said the central spring of movement was in the center of the back at the base of the spine, Isadora Duncan taught her pupils to "listen to the music with your soul . . . feel an inner self awakening . . . feel it is by its strength that your head is lifted, that your arms are raised, that you are walking slowly toward the light."

Duncan, invited by Pavlowa to see her work on the occasion of her first visit to St. Petersburg, wrote:

"I arrived to find Pavlowa standing in her tulle dress practising at the bar, going through the most rigorous gymnastics, while an old gentleman with a violin marked the time, and admonished her to greater efforts. That was the famous Master Petipa.

"For three hours I sat tense with bewilderment, watching the amazing feats of Pavlowa. She seemed made of steel and elastic. Her beautiful face took on the stern lines of a martyr. She never stopped for one moment. The whole tendency of this training seems to be to separate the gymnastic movements of the body completely from the mind. The mind, on the contrary, can only suffer in aloofness from this rigorous muscular discipline. This is just the opposite from all the theories on which I founded my school, by which the body becomes transparent and is a medium for the mind and spirit."

The Duncan School was started in Berlin with the patronage of a committee of very prominent and aristocratic women. It was a great success and so were Isadora's performances. The audiences came with religious fervor. At matinée performances the sick were brought on litters and went away in better health.

But after Isadora's love affair with Gordon Craig and the birth of their child Deirdre, the ladies of the Grünewald School Committee majestically withdrew their patronage. They could not support a school whose leader had such loose morals.

Isadora, indignant and undaunted, hired the Philharmonic Saal and gave a lecture on "dance, an art of liberation." She concluded the lecture with a talk on the right of woman to love and bear children as she pleased.

If she had only visioned the dance as a solo, as Isadora wrote, her way would have been quite simple in Europe. But she was possessed by the desire to create an orchestra of dancers, a chorus that would be to sight what the symphonies were to sound. Her pupils were learning to dance with such beauty that she determined to try to raise money to meet the expenses of the School by taking them to various countries. She hoped at least one government would recognize the value of her dance system for the education of children, and would invite her to establish a school. But this did not happen. The German Kaiserin was too Puritanical, the Prussian Regime too heavy to support a dance dedicated to free movement. The trip Isadora made to St. Petersburg in 1907 with a group of twenty pupils was not successful, although Stanislavski did all he could to help. The public, too, was enthusiastic about the Duncan Dancers; but the Imperial Ballet, the intrinsic expression of Tsaristic etiquette, was too firmly rooted to make any change possible.

Undismayed by her failure to win government support in Germany and Russia, the dancer and her little troupe went to England. Under the management of Charles Frohman they danced at the Duke of York's theatre in London for several weeks, and at the Duchess of Manchester's country house for King Edward and Queen Alexandra. Audiences and aristocracy were charmed; they pronounced the entertainment delightful amusement, but no real aid was offered to found the school Miss Duncan dreamed of.

So the troupe went back to Grünewald and Isadora Duncan, with no money left in her bank account, signed a contract with Charles Frohman for an American tour.

In her opening performances at the Criterion Theatre in New York in August, 1908, she danced Glück's *Iphigenie in Aulis* and Beethoven's *Seventh Symphony*. Isadora's own comments were as follows:

"In the heat of August, as a Broadway attraction, with a small and insufficient orchestra . . . the result was, as might have been expected, a flat failure. The few people who wandered into the theatre when the temperature was ninety degrees, and more, were bewildered and most of them not pleased. The critics were few, and wrote badly. On the whole I could not but feel that my return to my native country was a great mistake."

The *Sun* reviewed the performance favorably:

"She scored a most artistic success. She does not rely on physical charms as do some so-called dancers. Her success comes through grace and ease of movement, not her ability to kick or wriggle or do acrobatic tricks. The significance of her poses was probably appreciated by few in the audience, but the grace of posture of the dancer always appealed to the eye."

As in Europe, Isadora instantly commanded the passionate admiration and support of painters, sculptors and poets. George Grey Barnard came to every performance. George Bellows, Robert Henri, Percy MacKaye, Max Eastman, William Vaughn Moody, Edward Arlington Robinson, and Ridgeley Torrence came often. These "young revolutionaries of Greenwich Village" were Duncan worshipers, but their loyalty did not make her New York season a success. Audiences were small and cold and Frohman, recognizing that Duncan was not Broadway, decided to send her out on a six months' tour.

In Boston, Brooklyn, Buffalo, Philadelphia, Chicago, Syracuse and Rochester, music critics reviewed Isadora Duncan's dancing with favor.

Boston Transcript:

"She has studied the poses of Grecian Dancers on vases and the relics of antiquity and has reproduced these in a creative harmony of succession building up from the separate poses a series of dances. . . . In Miss Duncan's dancing there is the spirit of poetry of things suggested. There is no hint of the personality of the artist either in their tone of sensuous or sensual. The dancer's costumes appear merely a background for her art. The audience never centers its attention upon them to the exclusion of the dancer's theme."

Brooklyn Daily Eagle:

"Her dancing is at once a pantomime, a series of classic poses and a revelation of Hellenic Art."

Buffalo Express:

"Thinking over her performance one scarcely recalls whether she is beautiful or tall; one remembers only that she is a perfect exemplification of *human* grace, the *embodiment* of the poetry of motion. . . . It would be folly to dissect her work. One cannot put a sunset in words or set down in cold type the emotions aroused by a perfect statue. Miss Duncan's dancing equally defies description. She expresses beauty, simplicity, joy of living and the emotional freshness of that grace carved for all ages on some Attic frieze. . . ."

Philadelphia Telegraph:

"In this present day of elaboration and artificiality Miss Duncan's art comes as a pure breath from some pine-clad mountain height, refreshing as its ozone, beautiful and true as the overarching blue sky. Entirely simple, natural and unaffected, she presents a picture of beauty, joy and abandon as one believes it must have been when the world was young and youth danced in the sunlight for the mere joy of life."

Chicago Tribune:

"Her dancing is reverential in character, given to the world as artistic productions."

Syracuse Post:

"The fascination of Miss Duncan's exquisite movements lies in their perfect naturalness. Despite the years of careful conscientious work she has given to her art, there is nothing studied or stilted about it. . . . Every muscle of her body lends itself to the poetry of motion which she so charmingly realizes. Miss Duncan dances in bare feet and limbs but there is absolutely no suggestiveness in her movements, which are as chaste as they are classical in conception and execution. The matter of sex is entirely eliminated and one thinks only of the art which she illuminates. One seems to recognize her at once, not as a person but as a familiar figure often seen in painted colors or in marble. She seems less the individual and more the embodiment of artistic ideas."

Rochester, N. Y.:

"Miss Isadora Duncan is gone—but she leaves a memory which people will cherish . . . the fixed and mechanical steps of the modern dance are neglected; but their place is taken by the freer rhythm of the whole being. The modern dancer—your Taglionis, your Esslers and the rest, are not good to look upon; the lower limbs are overdeveloped to ugliness; the arms are relatively thin. That is the result of an art which, compared to the Grecian Art of the Dance, is as a rococo church is to the Parthenon. The audience watched the dancer with ever increasing pleasure. Miss Duncan conquered Rochester."

But the financial loss was tremendous and Isadora, blaming Frohman and out of patience with his comment that her art was considerably over the heads of Americans, that they never would understand it and that she had better return to Europe, tore up her contract.

Encouraged by George Barnard and in love with him, she decided to stay in New York, rented a studio in the Beaux Arts Building, installed her blue curtains, and set about creating new dances which she performed every evening for sculptors, painters, poets and musicians.

The *New York Sunday Sun* of November, 1908, described one of these evenings:

"She [Isadora Duncan] is swathed from the waist down in a wonderful bit of Chinese embroidery. Her short dark hair is rolled and coiled in a loose knot at the nape of her neck, parted simply, Madonna-like, about her face . . . and up-turned nose and greyish-blue eyes. Many of her press notices speak of her as being tall and statuesque—a triumph of art, for she is in reality but five-feet-six, and weighs one hundred and twenty-five pounds.

"Amber-hued lights are turned on, and a yellow disk in the center of the ceiling glows softly, completing the color effects. Miss Duncan apologizes for the incongruity of the piano music. 'There should be no music for such a dance,' she says, 'except such music as Pan might make on a reed cut from the river bank, a flute perhaps, a shepherd's pipe—that is all. The other arts— painting, sculpture, music, poetry—have left dancing far behind. It has been practically one of the lost arts, and to try to harmonize it with one so far ahead as music is difficult and inconsistent. It is to revive the lost art of dancing that I have devoted my life.'

"She has been standing near her parterre of poets when she begins to talk, and when she finishes, she is at the other side of the room. You do not know how she got there, but you think of her friend Ellen Terry as she does it, and the latter's nonchalant way of ignoring space.

"She is no longer a fatigued sad-faced hostess, but a pagan spirit,

83— C828

LIBRARY
ATLANTIC CHRISTIAN COLLEGE
WILSON, N. C.

stepping naturally from a bit of broken marble as if that were the most obvious thing in the world to do. A Galatea, perhaps, for certainly Galatea danced in the few moments of her release. She is Daphne with loosened hair, escaping the embraces of Apollo in that Delphic Grove. . . . Miss Duncan admits that her whole life has been an effort to go back, to discover that simplicity which has been lost in the maze of many generations.

" 'In those far-off days which we are pleased to call Pagan, every emotion had its corresponding movement,' she says. 'Soul, body, mind worked together in perfect harmony. Look at those Hellenic men and maidens caught and imprisoned by sculpture's lure, rather than hacked and chiseled from opposing marble—you can almost tell what they will say to you when they open their lips, and, if they do not open them, what matter, for you know just the same.' "

One day Walter Damrosch came to the studio. He had seen Isadora dance the *Seventh Symphony* of Beethoven at the Criterion Theatre with a small ill-trained orchestra. He proposed a series of performances at the Metropolitan Opera House. Miss Duncan accepted with enthusiasm and the concerts took place in December, 1908. These concerts were so successful that they were repeated on tour. Isadora interpreted the joy of Brünnehilde awakened by Siegfried, the soul of Isolde seeking realization in death, and scenes from Glück's *Orpheus*.

The Rev. Dr. Fayette Thompson, pastor of Lindell Avenue M.E. Church in St. Louis, in a sermon, delivered a scathing denunciation of Isadora Duncan and her dance performance in "conjunction with the Damrosch orchestra concert before a fashionable St. Louis audience at the Coliseum last Tuesday night." To his own congregation of people of wealth and fashion, some of whom were in the Duncan audience, Dr. Thompson said: "A virtually naked woman dancing before a great throng of people! Shame that such an exhibition was possible in this city!"

The Washington Methodist and Baptist ministers expressed themselves in similar terms, and without the favorable comment of President Theodore Roosevelt the tour might have ended less profitably than it did.

She returned to New York to find a healthy bank balance, however, and left for Europe to rejoin her child Deirdre and her school.

But the money earned "dancing and interpreting in pantomime three movements from Beethoven's Symphony No. 7, and Waltzes,

Preludes and Mazurkas of Chopin"* with an eighty-piece orchestra led by Walter Damrosch did not go far nor last long.

Confident her earnings in the United States and her triumph at the Gaiété Lyrique Theatre in Paris the winter of 1909-10 would assure the permanent establishment of her school, Isadora rented apartments in Paris for herself and twenty of her pupils, leaving twenty in Grünewald with her sister Elizabeth. At the end of the Paris season she was bankrupt again.

There was nothing else to do but to accept the help of a fabulous Lohengrin, who lived in Europe on the profits earned by his American factories, and true to character was bound to be the lover of the sensation of Paris. He carried her and her dancing school off to the Mediterranean, financed her return to America for a second tour with Walter Damrosch in 1911, gave her a son and would have married her if she had consented to sharing the domestic life of the rich.

But neither this episode nor the American tour ended happily. The millionaire Lohengrin fell ill of excess fortune and the press notices of the most distinguished critic in America—H. T. Parker of the *Boston Transcript*—forecast the beginning of the decline in the dancer's power; he noted the change in her leg and body that "suggests middle-age."

She danced a Bach-Wagner program at Carnegie Hall. An air, two gavottes and a gigue from Bach. "The Dance of the Flower Maidens" from *Parsifal*. "The Bacchanale" (Paris Version) from *Tannhäuser*, the "Liebestod" from *Tristan and Isolde*, and the "Dance of the Apprentices" from *Die Meistersinger*. Walter Damrosch's orchestral selections were from the same composers.

The critic of the *New York Evening Post* wrote:

"It can add no beauty to Wagner or to Bach to have their sublime thoughts illustrated by any dancer. To be sure the Bach numbers were dances, and so were the Bacchanale from *Tannhäuser*, the waltz from the third act of *Meistersinger*, and the scene of the flower girls from *Parsifal*. But these can all stand on their musical merits. A stageful of Pavlowas and Mordkins would be able to perform the Bacchanale as Wagner dreamed it; but Miss Duncan gives a very feeble idea of that wild scene. [She] reminded one quite forcibly of Marie Dressler in *Tillie's Night-*

---

* From the program notes of the performance at the Metropolitan Opera House, November 6, 1908.

mare. What have Greek poses, so called, and an abbreviated costume to do with the waltz from the *Meistersinger?* And mimetic illustrations . . . of Isolde's 'Liebestod' . . . which ended the program were too absurd for serious consideration."

Of her Boston performance Mr. Parker wrote:

"The social and aesthetic contingents that used to profess the utmost joy in Miss Duncan were lacking. . . . There was more applause for the performance of the prelude to *Lohengrin* played by Mr. Damrosch and his orchestra as an intermediate piece than there was for almost any of Miss Duncan's dances. . . ."

Seeming to regret his city's indifference, he writes his own impressions:

"She can still dance and mince with her old plastic skill, her poetry of imagination, her sublimation of motion . . . her newest venture has led her into the music of Bach and Wagner. Perhaps into both she tries to read too much. It is hard to draw from Bach's Suite in D, for example, another emotion than that of the beauty and interplay of patterns of sound. It is doubtful if the dance tunes were any more than dance tunes. . . . Miss Duncan seemed to care little for them as such; she tried to clothe them in her motions with a plastic imagery of her own, and it was not interesting. She succeeded much better with the 'Bacchanale' from *Tannhäuser,* the Dance of the Flower Maidens from *Parsifal* and the Dance of the Apprentices from *Die Meistersinger* because she danced them and translated and idealized as she danced. She was finely imaginative in her differentiation of the dances of *Parsifal* and *Die Meistersinger.* The music of the Flower Maidens is a subtle waltz of seduction; the music of the apprentices a frank waltz of youthful enjoyment. In the latter, conventionalized rhythms are etherealized into bright filaments; not the Nüremberg youth, but the youth of the Elysian fields, having heard the waltz tinkling from the earth, so transmuted it.

"In the Venusberg music from *Tannhäuser* the dancer seemed to be seeking a sensual grotesquerie. The spectator thought not of classic sculptures but of wall paintings at Pompeii in the decline of borrowed and debased arts. Wagner's music implies an orgiastic rout. No one but the stage manager is foolish enough to embody it in flesh and blood, color and motion. He must, since Wagner's equally foolish stage directions bid him do so. Every sensitive spectator shuts his eyes and sees in the music what he hears. Miss Duncan's dancing and mincing was quite of a lascivious rout of fauns and satyrs as Greek fancy liked to make play with them; but it was not at all of a romantically glamorous Wagner, or of her whose concern is ideal beauty. . . . She tries to do more with the music than she has ever done before; the result is less. Moreover, the conquering Russians have come and there were times last night when somehow the spectator saw Miss Duncan through and beside the beautiful phantom, as it were, of Anna Pavlowa. She was trained in the technique that Miss Duncan disdains, yet that technique, granted an equality of imagination and poesy, enables Miss Pavlowa to achieve a beauty and suggestion that Miss Duncan cannot reach . . . but there were moments, and sometimes long moments, when Miss Duncan attained the very beauty that she sought, when to watch it and her was an emotion in itself. Never before have some of her motions and poses so clearly suggested the Grecian marbles and vases she professes to study. Once and again, Diana of the Chase, for an instant, crossed the stage. Once and again, the eye seemed to see in some graceful circling of the arms, in some pure outline of the body, in some turn of head, throat, the very figures of the Hellenic women on the vases, immortal, by the paradox of everlasting beauty, in their day. Miss Duncan's head and throat have always had their beauty; last night, her play with them heightened it. She mimed less with her countenance than by them. Her arms, too, and her hands are capable of that wave-like grace which hitherto has been Miss St. Denis' peculiar possession."

Frederick Allen King whose *Pageant of the Dance in America* is a mine of recorded experience in the study and appreciation of the dancers who performed in the United States from the time of Vestris and Taglioni to the Works Progress Administration Dance Project in 1936, commented on Mr. Parker's critique as follows:

"Such words as these will tell posterity how it was that painters and sculptors saw in Isadora a new revelation, and that they more than musicians were her ardent admirers. This may not have been what Isadora sought as her time went on. It was her inner visions that she was eager to convey; and because the composers she used drew their inspiration from the same sources as she herself drew them—the earth and the elements—she came to cast aside her claims of inspiration from the Greeks and claim Walt Whitman and the great American reaches of lands, mountains and rivers."

John Martin wrote in 1939:

"She restored the dance to life. The body was no longer merely an instrument for the articulating of arms and legs in design and imitative gesture, but a totality of spontaneous expressiveness. In the development of movement thus from an inner source, *it was her ideal to find for every dance key moments,* from which other movements would flow of their own accord in fulfillment of the initial impulse. *Here was the discovery of the motor phrase* and the realization of the power of movement to evolve its own forms. . . ."

Fokine, in his reply to a charge made by Serge Diaghileff that Duncan's visit to St. Petersburg had reformed the Russian Ballet and that her influence on Fokine "lay at the base of all his creative work," wrote that he had started his revolutionary movement several years before he saw Duncan dance. He does not deny his admiration for her but he defines the different quality of his work and hers.

"She was for the freedom of the body from clothes; I am for the obedience of the costume to the movements of the body and its proper adaptation to the style of the period. She had one style of movement, one plastique for all periods and nationalities; I am interested in the difference of the movements of each individual person. She had the same form of dance for Wagner that she had for Glück, for Chopin, for the Spanish dances of Moszkowski and for the waltzes of Strauss. For me each period, each nationality and therefore each composer, requires an individual form of plastic movement. In Duncan's dances the national character is absent. Only Greece, ancient Greece, attracted her with its art, as if it were adaptable in its form to all periods."*

SUMMARY OF SIGNIFICANCE

To the audiences in America, the movement of Isadora Duncan's body in gesture and dance was a preparation for the dance idiom American dancers and choreographers would develop—an idiom which was to be a communication of the whole body; not of one or another of its parts. An idiom that was to affirm in time the wholeness, the one-ness of man the human being as opposed to man the social puppet or the slave of science.

Her one indispensable instrument was her beautiful body. With it she gave her audiences their emotions in human form, no invisible spectacle conjured by the mind out of memories recalled through the gallery of the ear. She incarnated music because she made sound into flesh.

This is not done without feeding the physical nature with a rich variety of sensations. The loves and lovers of Isadora Duncan were as indispensable to her art as consuming of her life.

She could not found a school. Hers was a personal communica-

---

* The *New York Times*, 1931.

tion of Physical Beauty, a living statement that man can not live on Science and Morality alone; that Truth and Good without Beauty distort the character and shape of men and women; that the physical enjoyment of Beauty, sensuous and sensual, there must be, whether for good or ill.

CHAPTER II

TED SHAWN

A PERSONIFICATION OF HUMAN STRENGTH SURMOUNTS
TECHNIQUE; MAN GREATER THAN MATERIAL

In his book, *The American Ballet,* Shawn wrote at the conclusion of the first chapter:

"We approach the dance as a thing of utmost importance—neither religious observances, nor political machines, nor educational institutions rank in vital significance with the way we dance . . . We must release, through the American dance, that spirit which would bear hardship, poverty and even death rather than submit to mental and spiritual tyranny."

A declaration of independence from human authority is only a short step from the creation of a mythology. In taking that step, Ted Shawn revealed his strength and his weakness. He was strong enough to break away from a weak and dangerous pattern of human authority. But he did not conceive and create the symbol of a just form of human authority with the instrument and materials at his command. He used the dance to destroy materialism, but he ended with supernaturalism. He deplored the worship of machines and machinery; he ended by exalting biceps and the athletic male. It remained for his followers to create a dance expression that revealed man possessed of human virtues, not of heroic qualities alone.

The first followers of Ted Shawn were a great multitude of American Anglo-Saxons who shared his dissatisfaction with the social order and the life of their time. They subscribed to the philosophy he stated as clearly in his dancing as in his books and lectures. Just as Duncan insisted on the classic principle that woman's first definition must be Physical Beauty, Shawn insisted man's first definition must be Physical Strength. He rejected a civilization that accepted shrunk shanks in its white collar workers, stooped shoulders, squinting eyes, puny arms in its laboratory men, dull, brute power in the industrial plant worker, harnessed to factory equipment, and the feeble attitudes of drug-store and drawing-room dandies.

Shawn was in revolt against the worship of material power and the submission of man to the machine. He taught his pupils to dance a dance he created in his films, in the vacation centers, to destroy "the false religion." They did. He created and they taught America to recognize the Hero and the God. His influence was great enough to counteract the effect of such "hard-boiled-school" writers as Ernest Hemingway and Erskine Caldwell, but his heroes and gods were regional only, inspired by race pride and a naive faith in geographical boundaries.

Like Hercules, Shawn labored and defeated many monsters, not the least of them the narrow conservatism that was strangling American education. But he failed in his task of ridding America of its narrow provincialism and arrogant regionalism. Yet, future dancers accomplished this task because Shawn made a way for them.

Edwin Myers Shawn was born in 1891 in Kansas City, Missouri. Most of his mother's family were show people; but Ted had entered a school of divinity and was studying to be a Methodist minister, when he fell ill of a severe attack of diphtheria in his junior year at the University of Denver. During the many weeks of enforced quiet, he says he had time to think deeply; he thought himself "out of the ministry, out of the Methodist Church, and free from all previous moorings."

It is interesting to have him recognize the fact that his inner spirit did not change with the change in his form of expression. Dancing took the place of preaching—that was all. The fundamental concepts of Protestantism had not altered within the nature of America's first great male dancer. He was inspired by Walt Whitman. But Whitman had done little else but adapt the style and form of the Bible to the vocabulary of the day. Whitman made religion sociology by providing sociology with a vivid language. The barren effort of calling sociology religion was never more evident than in the struggle Shawn made to evoke a mystic and beautiful ritual in his church dances.

He moved to Los Angeles from Denver, created a film, *Dance of the Ages,* for the Edison Company, which began with Neanderthal man and concluded with the latest ballroom steps.

He was sent on tour by the Santa Fé Railroad Company to dance the dances in the film in the vacation centers provided by them for their employees.

In 1911, at the age of twenty, he saw Ruth St. Denis' dance numbers from her first New York program of "Oriental dances" and parts of *Egypta.*

In 1914, he walked into her New York studio, talked to her for eight hours, and began the association which culminated in Denishawn and their marriage.

THE BALLETS OF TED SHAWN

Shawn wrote, "The obvious themes which first come to mind when one thinks of American art production of any kind are the Indian and the Negro," and further, "There is much more in the Anglo-Saxon history of America to produce dance themes than one might at first suppose," and further, "Spanish colonists . . . and the colonists from other nations are also a legitimate theme for research and production under the banner of American ballet . . . also in frontier and village life . . ." and "Our heritage of American literature is another vast field of dance inspiration, Whitman, the cosmic, Bret Harte for early California, Robert Frost for New England, Edgar Lee Masters for Illinois . . . the great American legendary hero, Paul Bunyan, Uncle Tom's Cabin," and also, "The abstract elements of America which must eventually find expression in the American dance. The rhythms of machinery . . . of motor transportation . . . of business commercialism . . . of our sports—football, baseball, rowing, tennis, golf—of our unique architecture out-Babyloning Babylon." But his own ballet ensembles, trios, duets and solos were not concerned for the most part with any of the themes listed above.

In a list of some sixty original works created by Shawn between the years 1911 and 1931, the following are the only ones inspired by the sources he enumerates in his chapter on American Thematic Material:

I. The Indian Source
   1. *Xochitl,* based on a Toltec legend. Music by Homer Grunn.
   2. *The Feather of the Dawn,* inspired by Hopi Ceremonial. Music by Charles Wakefield Cadman.
   3. *Osage-Pawnee,* a dance of greeting. Music by Ganne.
   4. *Zuni,* an Indian ghost dance. Music by Carlos Troyer.
   5. *Invocation to the Thunderbird.* Music by John Philip Sousa.

II. The Anglo-Saxon History of America. ("The English Colonists brought over their court and folk dances.")
   1. *Boston Fancy, 1854.* Music by Eastwood Lane.

III. The Frontier and Early Phases of American Village Life
   1. *Cowboy Tommy.*
   2. *Crapshooters.*
   3. *Dance Americane.* Music by Dent Mowry.
   4. Four Dances based on American Folk Music:
      a) *Country Dance*
      b) *Negro Spiritual*
      c) *Revival Hymn*
      d) *Battle Hymn of the Republic*

IV. American Literature
   1. *Jurgen,* a satiric ballet based on the novel by James Branch Cabell. Music by Deems Taylor. The program note said: "All moves uncomprehendingly. All my life was a foiled quest of you, Queen Helen. . . . Jurgen bidding farewell to that dream of beauty which he had the vision to see, but not the strength to follow."
   2. In collaboration with the composer, Eastwood Lane, a *Paul Bunyan Ballet* and *Sold Down the River,* a dance satire based on *Uncle Tom's Cabin.*
   3. *John Brown* and *O Libertad,* derived from Walt Whitman's *Leaves of Grass.*

V. The Rhythms of Machinery
   1. *Pacific 231.* Music by Honegger.
   2. *Geometric Dance.*
   3. *The Metal Dance.*

The most important of these works were *Boston Fancy, Cowboy Tommy* and *Dance Americane.*

The first encouraged Henry Ford "to bring on a New England dancing teacher and turn a floor of one of his factories into a dance hall," and *Cowboy Tommy* and *Dance Americane* framed a frontier character and a small-town "smart aleck," which later developed into epic and genre works of major importance by Eugene Loring, Charles Weidman and Doris Humphrey.

But Shawn's greatest work was not concerned with colonial, folk, genre or epic themes. Nor with war dances, which is probably as good a name as any for the rhythms of machinery.

His main interest was in religious dancing—"dancing and praying are the same thing"; in dancing for men—"the right of a boy or man to dance as an independent artist, not merely in the roles of comedian and acrobat"; and in "Denishawn," an organization of dancers, "the first such in history headed by two American born and trained choreographers, every member of the company American born and trained, using work of American composers and producing many 'ballets'* on indigenous themes."

Shawn's religious dances were composed on a number of themes—Pagan, Christian, Oriental.

1. On the Bible: *Miriam, Sister of Moses.*
2. On the Catholic Legend: *O Brother Sun and Sister Moon,* a study of St. Francis. Music—an old Gregorian Chant arranged by Respighi.
3. On Greek Religious Sacrifices: *The Mysteries of Dionysus.* A joint recital at the Greek Theatre, University of California, with Alfred Kreymborg.
4. On Egyptian Religious Ceremony: *The Priestesses of Isis.*
5. On the Protestant Church Service of Today in America: Shawn danced the Opening Prayer, the Doxology, the Gloria, an Anthem, the Twenty-third Psalm, a Sermon on the text, *Ye Shall Know the Truth and the Truth Shall Make You Free,* a Hymn, and a Benediction.
6. On Spiritual Healing: Shawn wrote a scenario entitled *Dance That Heals.*

* Mr. Shawn's own definition of "ballet" was "an organization of dancers."

In his religious dance, Shawn was challenging the priesthood of the established Protestant Church. He called the divorce of the art of dance from religion and religious expression illogical.

"There is a general admission on the part of the churches today that they are losing ground as far as their vital contact with humanity is concerned, and various ways and means are being tried to reëstablish that contact, but the church will never hold its place again until the clergy become artists or artists go into the church to revitalize it. The greatest sins which the church has committed have been artistic and aesthetic sins . . . in some of its doings today the church is an offense against good taste, against beauty and against every craving of the human soul to be fed of beauty.

"Theosophists have a saying that the artists of today are the priests of tomorrow at school. They believe that the new root race now being born in the world will have a religion the expression of which will take the form of art, and that those people who are now expressing themselves through forms of beauty will be the priests of this new religion."

Shawn was saying that the Protestant service had become dogma or sterile doctrine, that it must return to a simple primitive language if the Protestant Church would communicate with human beings and not die in dusty archives.

But Shawn himself did not develop his idea of a reform of the Protestant Church by dance ritual. His Protestant Church Service Dance was not repeated very frequently. He refers to a "root race," but he does not seem to have noted that the Protestant Church is dedicated to serving the God of a chosen people and that a change of language will not suffice to reform a narrow spirit.

In 1933, Shawn organized and set forth with an all-male group of dancers as a manifesto of the right of men to dance. The group danced *Kinetic Molpai* and *Labor Symphony*. These works were based on movements of workers in farms, fields and factories. The dancers were chosen from such groups of athletes as scout masters and gymnasium teachers.

Baird Hastings wrote:

"Shawn provided them with movement which was sufficiently colloquial to be assimilated by provincial audiences with minimum resentment. He lectured, he gave demonstrations, he insisted and he succeeded."

The Denishawn School, training ground of the Denishawn dancers, was created by Ruth St. Denis and Ted Shawn, but Shawn, who arranged schedules and taught most of the classes, was its real head. The first classes were held in Westlake Park in Los Angeles in 1915. Ruth St. Denis has movingly described in her biography the unpretentious beginnings of the School of American Ballet which was to have as great an influence in its way as the world-famous Russian Imperial Ballet School.

"And now began the immemorial hunt for the place to live and work. In our enthusiasm it was great fun. Each new house loomed up as the house we were looking for. But always when we got there the room was not big enough, the rent too high, or there was not enough space to build our outdoor studio . . . however, we did find a delightful old house. . . . We began to put our plans into action . . . a dancing platform over the tennis court.

"Ted, as usual, bore the full brunt of organizing and putting into form and order the ideas that we both had. We used to call ourselves 'Spirit and Form.' You can easily guess which was which.

"In reply to our first little catalogues, pupils came to us from all the near-by states. . . . The teaching system was largely evolved by Ted. Our attitude from the beginning was, as Ted so aptly put it, that *the dance is too great to be encompassed by any one system.* With us the development of the individual was foremost. When possible we gave a 'diagnosis' lesson to the incoming student in order to learn the technical and temperamental direction the student should follow.

"These were basic techniques which we felt were absolutely necessary; but, resting upon these techniques, the pupil was encouraged to experiment. . . . The whole articulation of the school was intended as food either for the student who merely wanted a deepening and releasing experience of life or for the definitely avowed dancer with a career before her (or him). Later on, as the school developed, we invited teachers of other systems to join our staff to enrich the whole learning of the school. During the fifteen years of the school they ran the gamut from a Dalcroze teacher to a Mary Wigman disciple, Hawaiian instructors and a Japanese Sword Dancer.

"That this system which is, as Ted has said, lack of system (since it embraced so many techniques and cultures) proved harmonious to the American spirit and youth; was witnessed in the following years when one considers the number of creative dancers who emerged from the walls of Denishawn."

It would rather seem that the school satisfied Shawn's desire to establish "a community of artists that functioned as a church, with a definite and recognized purpose of providing spiritual food as well as aesthetic satisfaction . . . an ideal institution . . . a place where life is lived as an art . . . where the teaching of dancing, if consecratedly pursued, will release and develop true religious consciousness."

Shawn created a cult and a church to confound the false religion and hierarchy he descried, but the works he created and the gods his followers have worshipped bow to Physical Strength and Beauty, to values as material as any served by Science and Industry and the Methodist Church.

He danced and his pupils danced odes in celebration of heroic virtues and mythological powers. He did not bother to study the society of his time, nor the character of the American Man.

His work exalted Man, or the caste of transplanted Europeans that conquered many nations of Indians, ruled a race of colored people and built an industrial empire.

Ted Shawn may be summed up as the Anglo-Saxon Hercules who defeated Vulcan and his forge and factory. To match the speed, the volume, the pace, the energy and inertia of a Machine, Man must become the master of the elements—one of the gods.

Shawn made the athlete greater than the engineer, the banker, the manufacturer, but he did not conceive of any lofty purpose nor of a human project a man of strong physique might serve. He admired an instrument; he did not seem to know what to do with it.

"Every nation in the world's history has expressed in dance what was its most potential characteristic." On the basis of Ted Shawn's work, that characteristic seems to be "pride of body."

In the 40's Shawn sold his farm headquarters, Jacob's Pillow, to a corporation that engaged him as managing director of a summer dance school and festival. He built the Jacob's Pillow Dance Festival into international repute where equal opportunity was given to a wide variety of dance styles of ballet, both modern and ethnic. Jacob's Pillow is an integral part today of the music and art schedules in the Stockbridge, Massachusetts, area.

CHAPTER III

RUTH ST. DENIS

THE SPIRIT AND WORSHIP OF THE FLESH

Isadora Duncan, in revolt against the decadence of the pretty precision dancing of courts and imperial ballets, created a dance that revealed Beauty in the form of Woman. Ruth St. Denis, in revolt against the smug, earthy appetite of American farm and townsfolk, their utilitarian conception of the female and her body, created a dance that informed the rural districts and the small towns from Maine to California that the spirit of the flesh was Woman and that it should be housed in a temple and served by a cult and a ritual all its own.

What Charles Baudelaire and Gustave Flaubert had said to the insufferable French bourgeois of the nineteenth century, Ruth St. Denis said to Main Street in the first quarter of the twentieth century. Nothing the writers wrote had such an effect as her dance. Nothing the Diaghileff Company performed reached the hundreds of thousands she did. Inspired by the poster art of an American advertisement, she and American business made an idol and statue of flesh in the person of American Woman. To quote from her prose-poem:

> "I, the Dancer,
> Bring my body
> To the feet of God."

It would be interesting to make a detailed analysis of Ruth St. Denis' productions and to determine how much of her art was revelation or pure dance, how much pantomime or wordless description of action by pose and gesture, how much theatrical showmanship of very high order—the evocation of mood by décor, costume and accessory.

40

In his book entitled *Introduction to the Dance,* John Martin wrote that the East "was the inevitable source of material for St. Denis, but that her dances were not simply Oriental dances, as she was eager that people should understand. They were the medium for a spiritual idealism." And elsewhere Mr. Martin wrote that "both Duncan and St. Denis trace their lineage back to the primitive dance of re-creation; Duncan's to that Dionysian outpouring of emotion which itself becomes the God, St. Denis' to the Olympian evocation of his presence by ritual and symbol. The former is purely ecstatic, the latter rather religious."

This writer prefers the word "pagan" for the dance of Isadora Duncan. The word "profane" seems the best definition of the dance of Ruth St. Denis; certainly her mockery of the Protestant and Catholic rituals was profane.

Two works by Ruth St. Denis, *Rahda* and *The Masque of Mary,* seem to have been inspired by an inability to reconcile carnal love and the principles of Christianity. Neither Christian Science nor the teachings of Gautama Buddha nor Japanese noh drama nor Hindu religious thought satisfied Ruth St. Denis, daughter of an improvident inventor whose prophet was Tom Paine, whose prop was Irish whiskey, and of a strong-minded New England Methodist woman who—discarding corsets, bustles, starched petticoats and hair-rats—wrestled all her life with the conflict inherent in the Bible. The God of Moses and the God of Love, how could they be reconciled in the life of woman? By a discipline Ruth St. Denis never accepted.

The following quotation from *An Unfinished Life* by Miss St. Denis is an illustration in point:

"My inseparable pal was a Roman Catholic. . . . I used to admire in a puzzled way the devotion which got her up in time for six o'clock Mass. She did this rain or shine, and then, apparently, dropped the whole matter. Of course she did no such thing. She carried at the back of her mind the comfort and sense of protection of church. Many times, in the midst of my intellectual wrestlings with matters which troubled her not at all, I envied her uncomplicated faith. On rare occasions when I went to Mass with her, I was seduced by the atmosphere and somber beauty into wondering whether I could sustain myself in my spiritual path without an organization to support me.

"The question has never been fully answered. Once . . . I was reading a description of Buddhism in Japan. It told of Buddhist temples with their wealth of beautiful images, of the quiet dignity of priests as they moved about the altars, of the perpetual rising of incense into the great shadows of the temple, of the ceaseless stream of pilgrims who laid a flower at the foot of the Buddha and murmured their allegiance to him and his teaching. I take refuge in Buddha. I take refuge in the Law. I take refuge in the Order.

"I was irresistibly drawn to this picture where so much beauty was mingled with such deep devotion, *but suddenly I realized with a shock that my intensely Protestant soul was getting the same satisfaction from this heathen religion that I would have gotten from the Catholic Church.*

"No one could possibly understand my strange sense of guilt, for under the guise of art I had been slowly brought into an atmosphere of unthinking reverence and blind devotion."

What inspired the composition of *Rahda* and of *The Masque of Mary,* their production, performances and development, are the more significant by virtue of the above confession. Miss St. Denis had a strong moral conscience and a Protestant soul. Her shrewd showmanship used whatever it needed, guilt or no guilt, and it would seem that Ruth St. Denis, pioneer, prophet and dancer, was lacking only in enough sense of humor to enjoy seeing her soul profit by her five senses.

THE EVOLUTION OF "RAHDA"

In 1904, on tour with the Dubarry Company, in which David Belasco was starring Mrs. Leslie Carter, Ruth St. Denis was bored. Just as Isadora Duncan had rebelled at dancing insignificant parts in Augustin Daly's Shakespeare Company, Ruth St. Denis balked at the routine of her two dance numbers, her "lovely Louis XV costume of blue feathers," her solo aria "to the little French tune of Amaryllis" which she was "allowed to sing" during one of the ensemble dances.

When the company arrived in Buffalo, seeking escape from the "unromantic" city, a sleet storm, the theatrical boarding house with its usual drab hall bedroom and dingy furnishing, Ruth went to the drug store for a soda. Above the fountain she saw a cigarette poster of Egyptian deities. The seated figure of a half-naked woman impersonating the Goddess Isis made Ruth St. Denis aware of what she wanted to do. The commercial drawing for a cigarette company expressed to her the whole story that was Egypt. She knew her destiny as a dancer had come alive.

"In this figure before me was the symbol of the entire nation, culture and destiny of Egypt. . . . It was however not merely a symbol of Egypt, *but a universal symbol of all the elements* of history and art *which may be expressed through the human body.* . . . I identified myself in a flash with the figure of Isis."

Ruth St. Denis began to work on the dance in which she intended to reveal the whole nation of Egypt, its culture, history, religion, and art of life, man's eternal search for "beauty and grandeur."

She did not realize that she was going to reveal the nature and character of the American people, of the American Woman in the age of industrial imperialism, of the march from the province into Rome.

By the time the Dubarry Company reached San Francisco, the various episodes of the dance *Egypta* were blocked out in detail. Ruth had found time to visit every library even though playing one-night stands, and the image of her dance was clear and well-defined; she was determined not only to learn how to translate that image into movement, but to familiarize herself with painting, sculpture, color, line, music, costuming, stage direction and lighting. She was not content to be a dancer.

It might be said she was too lazy to discipline herself sufficiently to express herself in dance without the assistance of costume, music, décor and theatrical effects. She created a pageant and a pantomime with skill and success. But it was spectacle, neither true dance nor drama.

In her own words she said:

"It must be remembered that my creative instincts were and at the same time were not those of the dancer. . . . I was unconsciously obeying an inward impulse and did not stop to analyze or separate my actions. But without any question, I was at that time a kind of dancing ritualist. The intensities of my spiritual life had found a focus of action in exactly the same way that another earnest young person would enter the church. I longed to translate into rhythmic patterns a spiritual significance."

The spiritual significance Ruth St. Denis translated was the transcending power of the five senses.

When the Dubarry tour came to an end, she left Belasco, determined to find some way of creating and producing the dance *Egypta*. A chance trip to Coney Island provided a new source of inspiration. The East Indian village imported by the owners of the Hippodrome, with its snake charmers and holy men and

Nautch dancers, had an effect on Ruth St. Denis similar to that of the advertisement of Egyptian deities. She decided to create a Nautch dance, try to find a vaudeville booking and, with the money earned, produce *Egypta*.

But when she began to look up material in the library for her Nautch costume, her interest began to shift from Egypt to the mysteries of Hindu religion. Nautch dancing girls led her to the Deirdassi temple dancers, then to the temples and inevitably to Rahda, beloved of Krishna, the god of love.

Miss St. Denis wrote:

"... This seeming shift of loyalties *involved no basic change. The image of Egypta had set into vibration an inward state that would inevitably express itself from a certain center and after a certain pattern ... it made no difference what. ... The race culture was what I transmitted through the dance.*"

This is a straightforward statement of imperial pride and ambition, of the exaltation of the individual by mastery of the cultures of all races and creeds.

Miss St. Denis was frank about her "meager" technical equipment by comparison with the "ballet girl" or "acrobatic dancer." She insisted that any technique is sufficient if it reveals the artist's thought. It is, therefore, perfectly in order to be more concerned, as we have been, with *what* Ruth St. Denis was saying than with *how* she said it.

In 1906, Henry B. Harris gave a matinée at the Hudson Theatre and invited the vaudeville managers of New York to come to see a performance of *Rahda*. The managers with their cigars and expanding waistcoats were impressed but cautious. "All right for Paris ... no good for New York."

The audience at Proctor's Twenty-third Street Vaudeville, where *Rahda* played a short engagement, was puzzled. Oriental dancing in 1906 was a frank display of muscle power; it whetted the physical appetite as the "bumps" and "grinds" of strip-tease artists do today. The solemn display of a beautiful body shamelessly nude for those days startled the customers at Proctor's. They did not know "whether to approve the audacity or resent the lofty conception," Caroline and Charles Caffin said of the Proctor engagement in *Dancing and Dancers Today*.

It is probable that the vaudeville audience which was won over gradually, as Miss St. Denis wrote, from suspicion to appreciation, recognized the understanding of itself that the dancer was revealing. Rahda with her slow movements, her lazy, sensual gesture, her suite of worshippers and servants, was a familiar type of American woman. A woman who not only wanted a man for her body but a swami husband for her soul; a vigorous woman of insatiable appetite and violent ambition, whose physical splendor had dried up her human feeling.

Then salon society took up *Rahda*. Twenty-four leading society ladies sponsored "the act." Mrs. Orlando Rouland rented the Hudson Theatre from Harris for a nominal sum and sent out the following announcement:

"The following ladies, appreciating the beauty of the Oriental dance of *Rahda*, will unite in giving a matinée for the pleasure of their friends at the Hudson Theatre on Thursday afternoon, March 22, at half-past three o'clock."

A list of the ladies' names followed and then, "Tea will be served in the foyer at five o'clock."

The scenario of *Rahda** was worked over and changed many times. Miss St. Denis described the performance of March 22 in her autobiography.

The first dance was *The Purda*. The curtains parted on Incense Music by Harvey Loomis. "Long spirals of incense rose from two great burners near the footlights. Presently an Indian woman slipped through the shawls to pay puja to her gods." She carried a tray of incense, raised it, laid down the tray, and with rippling arms became the spirit of the smoke.

Of this episode Miss St. Denis wrote:

"The rising smoke of the incense was to me a symbol of devotion, of prayer and meditation, of the surrender of self and the ecstasy of release, and I attempted to say with my rippling arms and my whole body what I felt in my heart."

The second dance in the program was the *Cobra*. It was a very short dance consisting of a pantomime with the arms, which represented snakes. Miss St. Denis entered in a scraggly wig and filthy turban, her arms wrapped around her neck. Merchants and brass sellers watched as the dancer took the cobras from around her neck and made them move to the sound of a flute. They

---

* The music was arranged from *Lakmé*.

crawled and writhed around the woman's body as she sat passive on a platform. When they struck with a hiss, the dance was over.

Ted Shawn commented in *Pioneer and Prophet:*

"The cobras lent themselves not only to imitators but also to cartoons. Hardly a cartoonist in America or Europe but had a try at it. The cobras were also painted and sculptured many times, the painting by Orlando Rouland and the bronze by La Chaise standing foremost."

The next episode was *Rahda.* The place was a temple. Worshippers and pilgrims gathered in the outer court before entering the temple. Presently, through clouds of incense, the doors of the sacred shrine opened and the form of the goddess was revealed. When Rahda descended from her pedestal, her worshippers understood that their goddess had taken human form to reveal a great message of truth. She conveyed it in a mystic dance, the meaning of which was: "Seek no permanent happiness in an impermanent world." By the impermanent world, Miss St. Denis meant the world of the five senses. Their gratification led to unfulfillment and despair. "Only through renunciation does the soul arrive at peace." In Rahda's dance the senses were symbolized by different objects: jewels for sight, bells for hearing, garlands for smell, a bowl of wine for taste; and to symbolize touch, Rahda kissed her own hands.

Rahda became the talk of the town overnight; the chit of an actress who had never even been a star, played to packed theatres in Washington, Boston, New York and then London. She was as successful in Europe as in the United States. The audiences enjoyed the delirium of the five senses so well-enacted by the goddess who bade her devotees renounce the material world.

The following words of Miss St. Denis give a curious insight into her character:

"Neither *Rahda* nor any of the other temple dances belonged in the theatre. I was dimly aware of this when I tried to invoke an atmosphere of worship through the incense burned before the performances; I knew it with increasing clarity when I found my audiences always responding with silence to these dances. Intuitively I tried to re-state man's primitive use of the dance as an instrument of worship, and the result was a profound evolution in myself but no answer to the question, What temple will receive these dances?

"I have always been an itinerant preacher, a sort of artistic

Vaslav Nijinsky. Sketched by Andrey Avinoff during a performance of *Schéhérazade. Courtesy Mme. Elizabeth Shoumatoff.*

Vaslav Nijinsky in *Giselle. Dance Collection, New York Public Library at Lincoln Center, Astor, Lenox and Tilden Foundations.*

Anna Pavlowa in *Chopiniana. Andrew Studios. Oliveroff Collection, New York Public Library at Lincoln Center.*

Michel Fokine as Perseus in *Medusa. Goodwin, 1918. Dance Collection, New York Public Library at Lincoln Center, Astor, Lenox and Tilden Foundations.*

Mikhail Mordkin in *Legend of Ayziade, 1911. Dance Collection, New York Public Library at Lincoln Center, Astor, Lenox and Tilden Foundations.*

Anton Dolin. *Maurice Seymour. Dance Collection, New York Public Library at Lincoln Center, Astor, Lenox and Tilden Foundations.*

Antony Tudor and Irina Baranova in *Gala Performance*. *Maurice Seymour. Dance Collection, New York Public Library at Lincoln Center, Astor, Lenox and Tilden Foundations.*

B. F. Keith. *Theatre Collection, New York Public Library at Lincoln Center, Astor, Lenox and Tilden Foundations.*

E. F. Albee with ladies at the new E. F. Albee Theatre. *Theatre Collection, New York Public Library at Lincoln Center, Astor, Lenox and Tilden Foundations.*

Tony Pastor. *Theatre Collection, New York Public Library at Lincoln Center, Astor, Lenox and Tilden Foundations.*

Florenz Ziegfeld. *New York Public Library at Lincoln Center, Astor, Lenox and Tilden Foundations.*

Isadora Duncan. *Dance Collection, New York Public Library at Lincoln Center, Astor, Lenox and Tilden Foundations.*

Ted Shawn in *Gnossienne. Dance Collection, New York Publc Library at Lincoln Center, Astor, Lenox and Tilden Foundations.*

Ruth St. Denis in *Bakawali*. *White Studios. Dance Collection, New York Public Library at Lincoln Center, Astor, Lenox and Tilden Foundations.*

circuit rider with no place to lay my head. The fault must lie in myself, and my purpose in writing my autobiography is to try to find out where the trouble lurks."

The moral and message of *Rahda* may not have been very clear, but its theatrical quality was unchallengeable. It changed the methods of Broadway musicals, something which was not to happen again until Agnes de Mille made the chorus girl a ballet dancer, thirty years later.

Charles Frohman's stage manager of musical comedies wrote, in reference to "the Hindu Dances of Miss Ruth St. Denis":

"This sort of dancing—the new sort—appeals to the higher senses and makes you think. It interprets beautiful things and can be as expressive as music or poetry. In all the musical productions that I am to make for the coming season, I am trying to approach this in my dances, *which will be more postures and pictures than actual dancing,* as we understand it. I am sure that the next season or two will show an entire change in the manner of dancing as introduced into musical pieces."

The description in any detail of St. Denis productions would fill a great many books; but none of them surpassed *Rahda* in popularity or significance. *Egypta, India, O'Mika* represented her passion for a larger life similar to and characteristic of the nascent imperialism of America. *The Masque of Mary,* her last important work, attempted to reconcile imperial ambition and selfless love. The doubtful merit of such a production has already been suggested.

In a summary of her accomplishment, Ruth St. Denis must be admired for her energetic common sense and realism. The middle class, grown rich and powerful, must proceed from the mastery of crafts and techniques to the worship of art; the middle class, dedicated to the cult of nature and the exploitation of the physical world in the name of science, must also worship nature in the form and flesh of woman. Woman was neither a thing nor a technique. This is what Ruth St. Denis expressed in her theatrical creations. She made the middle class take account of itself, and if the form she used was less dance than pantomime, more spectacle than ritual, it was nonetheless magnificent, poetic pageantry in the grand romantic style.

In 1940 Ruth St. Denis opened a school of Oriental dance with La Meri in New York. In 1960 and 1961 she returned to Adelphi College where she had originally established the dance department. She created a new department dedicated to the arts and religion. Sound movies were made of several of her works. Her active career continued into her mid-eighties. She performed, taught, filmed and lectured in New York and on tour. In 1963 Miss St. Denis toured the United States, at 85, as narrator of "America Dances" and as a dancer in *Incense*. What with her many activities, including television appearances, the public has seen Miss St. Denis dance for 70 years.

CHAPTER IV

MARTHA GRAHAM

AMERICAN ELECTRA

"To understand dance for what it is, it is necessary that we know whence it comes and where it goes. It comes from the depths of man's inner nature, the unconscious, where memory dwells. As such, it inhabits the dancer. It goes into the experience of man, the spectator, awakening similar memories."

This is the creed of a fugitive from life. Communication to and from the unconscious is the indulgence of fantasy. And fantasy of a grim and spectral nature is as much a part of Martha Graham as it was of Edgar Allan Poe.

The source of this flight from reality in Martha Graham is her concern with man. She dared leave Olympus and the Gods, the Temple and the Grove; she turned her back on the Heroic and the Bucolic. She came to earth and found man; but she could not accept his subject state.

She wrote that the reason for the appearance of the modern dance, its departure from classical and romantic delineations, was not an end in itself, but the means to an end; that it was not done "to dramatize ugliness or to strike at sacred tradition but *because the old forms could not give voice to the more fully awakened man.*"

Miss Graham did not define what she meant by the more fully awakened man. But it would seem from the context that she meant the Puritan, the man who had been ruined by the first World War, and that she wanted to express in dance what was happening to him, that she wished to make him aware of the fact he had lost his independence, that he had become the slave of industry and the servant of its machines.

Yet what a dancer writes is not the true story of her feeling; a dancer must be judged on his or her movement as well as on

59

choice of theme. What is communicated by Martha Graham's movement and the themes of her dance?

Her movement is not classic. It is "pre-classic." Like Duncan and St. Denis, she dismisses "toe-dancing" and conventional ballet technique. She makes strong violent movements of great power and unpleasant ruthlessness. These seem to express a fury and restlessness reminiscent of caged animals, or of herded and driven folk.

Is she reminding the Puritan who once lived in small towns and farms that the city is a walled camp or a court where men march or dance attendance on a patron?

Martha Graham was born in Pittsburgh, Pennsylvania, daughter of a doctor who specialized in nervous diseases. When she was eight years old, her family moved to Santa Barbara, California, where she came under the influence of Ruth St. Denis. After completing her high school course because her parents insisted she should, she returned to become a member of the Denishawn group.

Martha Graham stayed with the Denishawn Company four years. But in 1923, after the tour to London, she left. She has always said her training with Denishawn was irreplaceable, but that she felt she must find her own form of expression.

Her first independent venture was to join the Greenwich Village Follies. As Isadora Duncan and Ruth St. Denis had done before her, she played small parts in a commercial production under the direction of a successful show-man.

But a dance with a large veil, an Oriental number, and a Moorish number, satisfied her as little as the role of "a fairy" and that of a Louis XV soubrette had satisfied her great predecessors, and she accepted the position of dance instructor at the Eastman School in Rochester, New York, determined to find a contemporary idiom for the dance.

But neither the beauty of woman, nor her magic influence over the senses of man, were themes used by Martha Graham. At her first New York recital on April 18, 1926, an unsponsored production at the Forty-eighth Street Theatre which was lent to her by Al Jones, producer of the Greenwich Follies, it was evident a new theme was dictating a new technique.

The fragile quality of Martha Graham's movement and the pale color of Satie's music in *Tanagra,* a work performed for the first time at Miss Graham's 1926 recital, were plain statements of decadence. The body lacked strength in motion, the music was thin. The broad sweep of Duncan's lyricism, of the melody of Glück and the music of Beethoven and Brahms, the hot or sultry color of the St. Denis pose, had shrunk and faded. *Tanagra* was a loss of dimension. Miss Graham realized this. *Tanagra* was dropped from her repertoire and instead of fragile solos to the music of sophisticated continental composers, her programs began to include such bold innovations as:

Revolt, to the music of Honegger (1927)
Immigrant, Steerage, Strike, to the music of Slavenski (1928).
Four Insincerities
a. Petulance;   b. Remorse
c. Politeness;   d. Vivacity
to the music of Prokofieff (1929), and at her eighth New York concert on March 29 at the Booth Theatre:
Adolescence, to the music of Hindemith
Unbalanced, to the music of Harsanyi.

It is important to note that all these works were solos. To the writer, Martha Graham expressed a personal condemnation of certain conventions of contemporary fashion in manners and morals but, as yet, no affirmation of faith in a new order. It is impossible not to liken these solos to the monologues of Ruth Draper. They were cunningly contrived and brilliantly executed, but of narrow and special application only. The myopia, heartlessness and superficiality of the upper classes is not a big enough theme to occupy a great artist to the exclusion of all else.

Would this fine dancer be content to satirize and distort a sorry state of affairs because she could not conceive of a better one? Would the decadence of a class be the predominant subject of her dance?

Martha Graham has been called austere, a Puritan, a prophet, and by Uday Shankar and Leopold Stokowski "an avatar," a dancer "whose motivation transcends a local idiom and expresses a planetary idea."

Leopold Stokowski believed Miss Graham stepped from the American scene into "lucid abstraction where one can feel one's own mind pushing against the horizon of its limitations and expanding in a new and altogether stimulating manner."

Whether it is possible to feel abstraction, and whether the mind has any understanding of human sentiment or is a method of direction of an ambition or a purpose, must be answered by the audience who attend the dance concerts of Martha Graham.

Martha Graham and her group made their debut at the Booth Theatre in New York in April, 1929.

At this, her ninth New York concert, the program included *Vision of the Apocalypse,* to music by Reutter, *Rustica,* to music by Poulenc, *Sketches from the People,* and *Heretic,* to an old Breton song.

Vision of the Apocalypse, the first work for a large group, was a dance pantomime on a theme and variations inspired by the Book of Revelations and the vision of a young monk. The vision was that of "the woes of man and the burden of his sins." The variations deal with Vision, Toil, Famine, Blasphemy, Ruthlessness, Pestilence, Mourning, Prayer and Death.

Miss Graham was not content to create dances of heroic and mythological character as Shawn did, or to become a profane priestess like Ruth St. Denis. She suffered torment, was beset by a sense of sin, and finally escaped into satire, a frenzied criticism of the society she could not resign herself to quit. For in spite of her brilliant and ruthless caricatures of the vices and follies of the American aristocracy in such works as *Punch and the Judy* and *Every Soul Is a Circus,* and her attempt to introduce Christian symbols in dance suites about the primitive religions of North American Indians as in *Primitive Mysteries,* Martha Graham made no affirmation of understanding in terms of humanity.

She used her group as she used her own body, to create a design of terror, or of grotesque self-abasement, martyrdom or persecution as powerful as it was crude and consciously ugly.

Her work pronounced the fate of those who reject the human, who prefer the worship of physical beauty, strength and mind. The dominant and terrifying theme of Martha Graham's dancing and pantomime was that of a small, plain woman driven by a powerful mind and a fierce will to fight for a place in a world where the coquette and the courtesan were the queens. She represented in her movement and gesture the agony of an intellectual who was helpless in a competition with physical beauty and sensuous values.

Inevitably, her compositions became less and less dance; they represented an absence of feeling, a numb rigor. Martha Graham became a cult. She was the idol and image of the bluestocking, the college graduate, the school teacher, the stenographer; of the woman who was neither blonde nor buxom, nor coy and arch, who was scribe and slave of a boss-man eight, ten or twelve hours a day, whose nights, holidays, and Sundays were spent washing, mending and pressing—alone, or with her like.

No review of Martha Graham's repertoire could omit her preoccupation with Americana. Under this heading come the following pantomimes, dances and dance dramas:

1. *American Provincials.* Music by Louis Horst.
   1. Act of Piety (Solo)
   2. Act of Judgment (Martha Graham and Group)
                    November 11, 1934
                    Guild Theatre, New York

2. *Frontier* (Solo). Music by Louis Horst.
        An American perspective of the plains.
            Décor by Isamu Noguchi
                    April 28, 1935
                    Guild Theatre, New York

3. *Panorama.* Music by Norman Lloyd.
   1. Theme of Dedication
   2. Imperial Theme
   3. Popular Theme
            Setting by Arch Lauterer
                    August 14, 1935
                    Bennington, Vt.

4. *Horizons* (Martha Graham and Group). Music by Louis Horst.
   1. Migration (New Traits)
   2. Dominion (Sanctified Power)
   3. Building Motif (Homesteading)
   4. Dance of Rejoicing
            Décor by Alexander Calder
                    February 23, 1936
                    Guild Theatre, New York

5. *Chronicle* (Martha Graham and Group)
   1. Dances Before Catastrophe
   2. Dances After Catastrophe
   3. Prelude to Action

Décor by Isamu Noguchi
December 20, 1936
Guild Theatre, New York

6. *American Document* (Martha Graham and Group)
Music by Ray Green
Costumes by Edythe Gilfond

7. *Every Soul Is a Circus* (Martha Graham and Group)
Music by Paul Nordoff
Setting by Philip Stapp
Costumes by Edythe Gilfond
December 27, 1939
St. James Théatre, New York

8. *Letter to the World* (Martha Graham and Group)
Music by Hunter Johnson
Setting by Arch Lauterer
Costumes by Edythe Gilfond

The background of *American Provincials* is the world of Hawthorne's *The Scarlet Letter.* John Martin wrote of this dance in the *New York Times:*

"A mighty and terrifying holiness is invoked with heroic frenzy. Departure on the part of one from tradition results in a ferocious condemnation, part sex, part pride, all demoniacal."

Barbara Morgan wrote:

"*Frontier,* subtitled *American Perspective of the Plains,* is a tribute to the vision and independence of the pioneer woman. It portrays her strength, and tenderness, her determination and jubilation at overcoming the hazards of a new land, as well as her love for the land. The movement, completely one with the décor's widening horizon, evokes the feeling of distance, loneliness and courage. *Frontier* is an American classic. It is as closely identified with Martha Graham as the *Swan Dance* was with Pavlowa.

"*Panorama.* This was the first Workshop Production of the Bennington School of the Dance. It presents three 'basically American' themes: the fanaticism of the Puritans in their hymn of dedication of a New World; the imperialism that enslaved a people 'in a Southern locale'; the awakening social consciousness of the contemporary scene.

"*Horizons.* Themes of Exploration and Discovery abstracted from the American background. Alexander Calder's Mobiles were used as moving décor to enlarge the sense of horizon.

"Chronicle. The composition (divided into four actual dances):
1. *Spectre and Masque*—1914
2. *Steps in the Street* and *Tragic Holiday*
3. *In Memoriam*
4. *Prelude to Action*

is a vibrant commentary on war and its destruction, not a war or *the* war, although the program indicates a 1914 derivation, but the looming horror of a universal catastrophe and its moral break-up. Here we have Miss Graham undertaking her largest theme and getting away, temporarily, from the court calendar.

"A just discussion of the movement in *Chronicle* would require a detailed description of the changes in each section. Miss Graham has incorporated in the work a tremendous variation in pattern, in fact, so extensive that the technique involved is one of the outstanding features of the dance, playing a greater part than her movement usually does in relation to the dance's content.

"It is concerned with the ugly logic of imperialism, its need of conquest, the inevitability of conflict, its rooted evil, and the approach of the masses to a logical conclusion. It shows the brutalizations of conquest, the hypocrisy of imperialism, the marching of men without cause, without direction, masking of the memory of conflict with memorials and the taut gathering of new energies and new forces."*

American Document—A Documentary Dance. "Our documents are our legends—our poignantly near history—our folk tales. The form of the piece is patterned freely after an American minstrel show."†

Words are spoken on the stage by an interlocutor. The quotations include passages from the Declaration of Independence, a letter from Red Jacket of the Senecas, Lincoln's Gettysburg Address, the sermons of Jonathan Edwards, the Song of Songs and Walt Whitman.

Every Soul Is a Circus. A satire inspired by the poem of Vachel Lindsay of the same title. The central character in Miss Graham's interpretation was "a silly woman" who is an appreciative spectator of her own behavior.

Letter to the World. A dance about the personality of America's greatest woman poet. The title and the spoken words that accompany the dance are from the poems of Emily Dickinson.

* From *Martha Graham* by Barbara Morgan, 1941.
† From the program notes.

The heroine of this work is the opposite of a "silly woman." The loss of her lover makes a woman face her destiny as an artist "with the realization that her happiness must be found in the intensity of her work" (Barbara Morgan). But this is an answer that Protestant and Puritans should accept joyfully. Art is work well done; and work is the God to whom Protestants and Puritans sacrifice themselves without reserve. They worship work; why should they seem frustrated and troubled? Is it because they are afraid to admit that the workshop of work is the worship of self?

Miss Graham's prevailing theme and its demonstration in her dance was that of an unhappy woman. Her subject matter and her movement were those of a hungry creature tormented by unfulfilled desires and ungratified appetites.

The following article is a comment on Martha Graham by Michel Fokine:

PATHETIC ART*

by MICHEL FOKINE

When Margarete Wallman came to America to promote the art of Mary Wigman, she called her teacher a "dark soul." She explained that this art portrayed in itself the depressed feeling of a Germanic soul after a lost war. When the critic, Stewart Palmer, discussed Miss Graham's work in the *Dance* Magazine, he also called her a dark soul.

America did not lose the war, and I do not know how to explain the sorrow of Miss Graham about which the magazine says "that before, she used to be a normal and pleasant girl." I think, simply by copying, by getting under the foreign influence. This is a transplanting of the sick art of Germany in the healthy America. [But Mr. Fokine does not realize that the Puritan class, to which Martha Graham belongs, did lose the war.]

But I have another explanation. The expression of sorrow in dance needs very little motion. It seems very easy. The expression of joy, however, needs a lot of movement. This is more difficult. The more happy we feel, the more we feel the necessity of movement.

The dance is mainly the pronouncement of joy and sun, not darkness. Certainly, the sad, like any other feeling, might be a subject of dance expression, but it is not the sorrow but the happiness which gave birth to dance, and this is joy which will lead it to a permanent development.

---

* *Novoye Russkoya Slovo*, March 1, 1931.

Pavlowa danced many quick joyful dances. On this road there are very few people who follow her, but there were many who tried to do *The Dying Swan,* because it seemed to be so easy. At one time there was no dancer, not a dancing child, who did not try to do the *Swan.* The great Duncan gave in her dances the whole scope of human emotions, but when I think of her followers, I see a picture of a virgin putting her hand on her head much in the manner of a figure from funeral processions from a Greek vase. The amateurs, in a very greedy way, throw themselves on things which are easy to execute and go on the line of least resistance. This observation of mine seemed to me especially true when I visited a few lectures in a school of social research conducted by John Martin. My last visit there was on the twentieth of February, and about this I want to say a few words.

Miss Graham was talking when I came in. Behind her were two rows of girls sitting on the floor in knitted sweaters. The platform for demonstration was in the middle of the room, and around the platform the audience. Miss Graham looks like a fanatic prophet. All her exterior seems to be fundamentally denying the smallest sign of coquetry, womanhood or beauty: a long tunic, very tightly slick combed hair, a bent spine, outspread tense elbows, shoulders bent forward, clenched fists or outspread fingers. . . . Everything tells us that she has risen above the old understanding of beauty and grace, that she is fundamentally denying them.

In explaining her theory, she often pointed with her hands to her bosom or her stomach and, as I gathered, there lay the center and the secret of her "new" art. Miss Graham all the time was interrupting her speech with the phrase, "Maybe someone would like to help me by asking me some questions?"

Questions followed and the lecturer immediately answered. There were questions of the following character: Is it necessary to be born for this specific art, or can it be acquired, not being especially born for it? Miss Graham immediately consoled her questioners: her girls possess the most different and varied temperaments, each one has her own personality, and yet they all conquered this art. I decided to ask no questions, although for me everything here was questionable.

The demonstrations of the dance continued. The girls lay down, sat down, walked on flat feet, and . . . that was all. The arms either hung limply or tensely pushed upwards with their elbows. The chest was always pushed out exaggeratedly or else was sharply sunk in. In these two movements was the essence of the dance. The tempo was only slow. The expression was sad, and almost always evil. Clenched fists. A somewhat barking movement of the torso and the head. The barking girls! . . . This is not only the cult of sorrow, it is the cult of evil, I thought. I pitied the young girls who deformed their bodies and, what is even more, deformed their souls.

All that I saw was monstrous in its form and evil in its content. The legs were placed arbitrarily with the feet pointing inward.

I looked around at the audience. Everyone sat in a simple and natural position. Each woman, whatever age, appeared an example of beauty or naturalness and truth, in comparison with what I saw in the middle of the room.

Presently a woman asked the following: What is Miss Graham's opinion of the ballet?

I was on the alert. Miss Graham replied that she recognized the ballet as one form of the dance, that she liked, for instance, Pavlowa, especially when Pavlowa, after each of her numbers, took a bow.

"She bowed very well. . . ." It is not hard to imagine what I felt after such a pronouncement of one of our greatest dancers, who had just died, dear to us all, Pavlowa! . . . The best thing that Pavlowa ever did was to take good bows. . . .

The lecturer continued. . . .

But when the ballet begins to approach the Grecian dances, it becomes "horrible"! She never once described why it was horrible, and the audience accepted her word without question, and some of them even applauded. I can not keep quiet, I said to myself, and continued to be silent. Others continued to ask questions and I kept quiet. But it seems that my face expressed more than I wanted to show, because Miss Graham turned to me.

"It seems you have a question . . . ?"

"Yes," said I, "will you be so kind as to explain this question? In working with your girls, do you have in mind the development of natural movement, or do you disregard naturalness in your art?"

Long, long silence. . . .

To all the other questions the answers had followed immediately.

"Must one be born for this dance or not?" This was settled in no time; but a question about the relation of the art of dance to natural movement and . . . the silence followed.

The cause of the embarrassment was understandable. All that had been demonstrated was to such an extent unnatural, to such an extent against nature, that there was really no possibility of speaking about the connection between life and this kind of "art."

A very foggy discussion followed the pause.

I repeated the question, and to make it more clear, asked permission to illustrate my point by gestures.

"It seems to me that your girls, in order to raise the hand, first of all raise their shoulders, then their elbows, and only then the whole arm. In life, it happens otherwise. If I want to take a hat from the hanger, I do not raise first my shoulder, then my elbow . . . no. I simply raise my whole arm and take that which I need. But according to your system, one must do exactly the opposite."

I showed how the simple movement would be performed according to the system of Miss Graham. It was funny. The public laughed, and so did Miss Graham and I.

"But I still insist that you do raise your shoulder in order to raise the arm," said she.

"I? Never."

She again referred to the place between the chest and the stomach.

"Is it from here that your movements originate?" And I also pointed to my stomach, reassuring myself that nothing extraordinary happened there when I took a book from the shelf.

"But you breathe?" she said.

"I always breathe," I said with conviction, to the accompaniment of laughter. I repeated my first question; I insisted on keeping it foremost in my approach to the lecturer, for the simple reason that it is impossible to find a better way of showing the difference between beautiful and ugly movements, between the clumsy and the graceful, than in the example of everyday gesture and everyday movement.

If a person is forced to rock his whole body in order to make a step, then we call him clumsy; if in order to pick up a light object he must tense his neck and those muscles which are not used in the movement, then we feel that he is not agile, is undeveloped of body; if he, in order to shake your hand, raises his shoulder and his elbow, rocks from one side to another, certainly he creates a very coarse impression. Movement becomes more beautiful the less we feel the tenseness in its execution. Such is the aesthetic of the ballet, such is the aesthetic of any dance. The teaching of the dance is based mainly on constant elimination of unnecessary tenseness.

The theory of Wigman and Graham is exactly the opposite. They seem to say: Be tense as much as you can. Without clarifying the question about natural movement, Miss Graham unexpectedly said:

"You know nothing about the movement of the body!"

Receiving from a young dancer such a compliment, and answering that I had been concerned with this question for more than forty years, I asked:

"May I ask another question?" The answer came less willingly than before.

"Did I understand correctly that all the movements are divided by you into two categories . . . those with the chest pushed out and those with the sunken chest?"

"Yes."

"Is it true that the chest expresses, in your opinion, anger and hatred?"

"Yes."

Here I thought of how we approach the bed of a dying man.

We pull the chest in, and this expresses the sorrow we feel, not hatred.

"Can I ask another question?"

"No," said Miss Graham, "we will never understand each other. Besides, it is not very nice of you to stop the lecture by your questions."

This was the second compliment I had received from the dancer.

"Why is the ballet horrible?" I asked nevertheless.

I had to repeat the question twice. Miss Graham assumed the fifth position, and thinking that this was very balletic, said:

"How can anyone dance the Greek dances in this fashion?"

"You know very little about the ballet," I said. "You don't know about the many existing ballets which are not built around the five positions, but in which every movement is built on natural expression, on purely Greek lines and style. You are criticizing the ballet without knowing it. . . .

"I myself have choreographed five to seven ballets and many of them in the Grecian style, for instance, *Daphnis and Chloe, Narcisse and Echo,* etc. Nijinsky has done *Afternoon of a Faun,* Pavlowa was famous in *Bacchanale.* Is it possible that all of this does not entitle me to a question . . . why the ballet is becoming horrible when it treats the Greek subject . . . why the monopoly of Greek dances must belong to the dilettanti?"

To my mind, even to call these dances as opposed to the ballet, seems false. Ballet is an art like music and painting, and modernism is a temporary condition, a period of evolution in art. The Diaghileff ballet, for instance, or Rolf De Maré's Swedish ballet, were so modern in some of their last works that the German dancers or modernists like Graham are left far behind.

But Miss Graham seems to know nothing either about modernism in the ballet or the ballets of Grecian style. If a dancer, an "intellectual," who talks more than dances, did not bother to study thoroughly the history of dancing, the history of everything which was done before her, and assumes that the ballet is only "the five positions," with the legs turned out, that is what I can not understand.

Here my identity was disclosed by someone in the audience and Miss Graham said, "I did not know I was speaking with Mr. Fokine."

I do not know how she would have spoken to me if she had known who I was. The fact remains that she finished the lecture and demonstration, her last words being:

"We will never understand each other."

I understand and love art of all the nations, no matter how remote, and of all the times. It is strange that I should not be able to understand the art and theory of Miss Graham.

CHAPTER V

DORIS HUMPHREY

THE OLD TESTAMENT IS NOT CHRISTIANITY

Neither Beauty nor Physical Stature, not Lust of Flesh, nor of Fame and High Place, these the Gods of Duncan, Shawn, St. Denis and Graham, concerned Doris Humphrey.

Hers was a grave and passionate search for truth, a faith in justice, an infinite pity for humankind and for its tragic and feeble creature—man.

Doris Humphrey, "the first choreographer of her time, marked the coming of age of the American dance. Here for the first time the dance took a heroic theme, the relationship of man to man, and treated it heroically in terms of an abstraction as pure as that of music, developing its material at length according to its demands of internal organization, and abandoning story sequence, impersonation and musical formalism altogether." This was the comment made by John Martin in his *Introduction to the Dance*.

Miss Humphrey, a descendant of Elder Brewster and Ralph Waldo Emerson, was born in Chicago. Both her grandfathers were Congregational ministers. Her mother was a pianist, her father a photographer. Her first teachers in the dance were Mary Wood Hinman (1905-10), Josephine Hatlanek (1909), and Pavlek and Oukrainsky (1912).

Doris Humphrey was still a school girl when she composed her first ballet, a long, ambitious work, entitled *Persephone and Demeter*.

The classic myth tells of Demeter, goddess of the fruitful soil who, in anger and despair when the god of the underworld carries off her daughter Persephone, made barren the earth until it was agreed Persephone should spend two-thirds of the year with her mother.

71

In the choice of this myth, which is the imaginative Greek way of expressing the irreconcilable conflict between nature and science, between the principle of growth and that of measure, between life and living and a cold abstraction, Doris Humphrey raised the foremost problem of our time.

But she not only reminded us in this work that the conflict between the physical elements of nature and the abstract principles of science was not a new one and that it had occupied the pagan mind of Greeks; this work, she wrote, started her on her path. That path led her, twenty years later, to the conclusion we found in *Inquest*, which may very well be one of the greatest American dance works composed by an American. Its theme, that of Christian faith in the brotherhood of man, denies effectively the power of science and pagan virtue over human love and affection.

Doris Humphrey was the fulfillment of the promise made by Isadora Duncan and her successors. The American dance began by insisting on the beauty of the feminine form; in Shawn it recognized the heroic quality of male strength; in St. Denis the voluptuous power of the flesh; in Graham the defeat of worldly ambition. Not until Doris Humphrey could our dance, which in technique must be described as "pre-classic," be said to express more than a race or a caste feeling. It took three hundred years to free us from the pattern imposed by the Elizabethan masters who launched the Massachusetts Bay and the Virginia colonies. Puritan and Cavalier principles struggled to administer the United States long after industry had created a world empire.

That neither class nor race may rule over humanity is a principle the leaders of this country have found hard to accept. It is the duty of the artist to lead the way from ignorance to understanding. Few American poets, painters or musicians have had so much vision and expressed it so eloquently as the dancer and choreographer Doris Humphrey.

Miss Humphrey's own account of the creation of *Persephone and Demeter* is the best:

"It was a fairly long ballet which I composed when I was seventeen, and just out of high school. It followed the original myth very closely, and had as much Greek flavor as I had been able to acquire in very brief experience. This was limited to some 'aesthetic' dancing, vaguely Duncan, and some knowledge of Greek art, and some ballet, which was, of course, not Greek. The theme intrigued me, however, as I loved the symbolism of it as a fertility rite, and the dramatic lines, and I felt no inadequacy as a choreographer at seventeen! I selected the music from pieces my mother knew. I remember my favorite was the 'waiting' motive from *Madame Butterfly*, which I used for Persephone's lament in the underworld! My mother and I dyed and made the costumes for the dancers, who were local young girls without much training, and I was Persephone. As I remember, everybody thought it was lovely, and it started me on my path, I think, as the only other dance I had composed before was a sort of Greek ritual, which still appears in Mary Wood Hinman's book of dances and music for teachers. . . ."

In 1914, she began to teach classes in Oak Park. Kohler, the bathroom fixture designer, was one of her star pupils. Urged by Mary Wood Hinman, she entered the Denishawn School in 1917, and in 1918 was invited to join that company.

Ruth St. Denis described Doris Humphrey's arrival at the Denishawn School very entertainingly:

"When Doris appeared for her first lesson in the little tent theatre at West Lake Park, she was a slender, prim young person, every inch the lady, wearing a preposterous pompadour and a bathing suit with a skirt, that daring costume which we had evolved for practice. She had come to us from Evanston, Illinois, where she had her own dancing school, in which a devoted mother helped her. But being a keen-minded young person and feeling that we Denishawns had some new note to add to her concept of the dance, she had packed a suitcase, and here she was. Watching her day by day, seeing the clean-cut, lovely execution of her bar work and her freer, more individual movements during our school recitals, it began to dawn on me that Doris was on the wrong track in clinging to teaching as the limit of her powers, and I said to her, 'You should dance. You can teach later if you want to, but you have the makings of a real artist. Think it over.' She did, and she began her steady and inevitable rise."

In Hollywood, at Krotona, the headquarters of the Annie Besant branch of the Theosophical Society, Doris Humphrey helped Ruth St. Denis create a ballet of the temptation of Buddha for the religious festival conceived by Mrs. Christine Wetherill Stevenson and Mr. Warrington, head of the Krotona Institute. Walter Hampden impersonated the Buddha, Ruth St. Denis played the part of the astral body of Yashodara, the wife, "who in the last desperate appeal of the heart, seeks in a lovely emotional plastique to bring the Buddha back from his austere heights to the warm loveliness of her arms." Doris Humphrey danced the interpretation of the god Kama.

Soon after the production of the ballet about the temptation of Buddha, the concept of dance as music visualization took shape in the mind of Ruth St. Denis. She organized a group of girls headed by Doris Humphrey to work on ensemble forms. Doris, said Miss St. Denis, was really her first co-creator; but from the very beginning, the pupil surpassed her teacher in the creation of choreographic forms of expression.

The first number produced by the girls' group was Beethoven's *Sonata Pathetique.* Miss St. Denis called it the first suggestion of what became the American Dance. A group of young women became, for the first time, simple instruments for music to play upon. A group of young American girls submitted their bodies to the passive expression of mood, emotion and physical experience dictated by the composer of a piece of music.

This concert dance not only defied Calvinism and contemporary conventions, but it challenged the principles of every feminist, every agitator for "women's rights," every blue-stocking, and every school-marm, whether masculine or feminine. It was the forerunner of the syn-choric or musical instrument ballet and the statement of a new faith in human as against artificial or abstract symbol of life and feeling.

The music visualization concert dance created by St. Denis and Humphrey differed from Isadora Duncan's dancing of Schubert, Beethoven and Glück in that the former maintained a consistent visualization of the structure and rhythm, whereas the latter was a personal, intimate and romantic expression.

Isadora Duncan had interpreted symphonic music in great solo dances. Denishawn went further. The ultra personal and romantic style was replaced by a more objective and abstract expression, but Denishawn could not accept realism; and for that reason Doris Humphrey and Charles Weidman, feeling the need of exploring in new fields, left Denishawn in 1928 and founded their own school.

Miss Humphrey's outstanding concert dances were *The Shakers, New Dance, Theatre Piece, American Holiday, With My Red Fires, Race of Life,* and *To the Dance,* which was awarded a national prize by *Dance* Magazine for the best group composition of 1938.

But what of the years that followed her break with Denishawn?

Was Ruth St. Denis correct in fearing the influence of Mary Wigman and the German School, those "sadly earth-bound" artists whose social consciousness dismayed the elegant adoration of Beauty practiced by Transcendentalism of Miss Ruth?

The early compositions of Doris Humphrey did not concern themselves with sociology.

Color Harmony abstract, based on the Young-Helmholz theory of light, regarded by John Martin as the beginning of the modern dance ensemble in this country, was a study in the terms of physics, or natural forces.

Water Study, composed in 1928, without music, based on the movement of the waves, included in *Americana*, 1932, was no statement of social consciousness. Not until the *Life of the Bee* with its dramatic presentation of the ferocity of the female of the species were we aware that the choreographer was concerned about the relations of living creatures to one another.

In October, 1928, she and Charles Weidman opened their own studio.

"Realism separated from actuality," was John Martin's definition of Doris Humphrey's dances, in his review of her performance of *Life of the Bee* at the Guild Theatre in New York, 1929.

This work, which followed *Water Study*, listed by Miss Humphrey as early composition, won high praise from the nation's first dance critic.

Life of the Bee was danced by an ensemble of fourteen who had worked together with Miss Humphrey for a year and a half. No member of this ensemble earned much money, fame or personal recognition. They appeared no more than four or five times during the season. Yet, to the mind of John Martin, they became the peer of the Diaghileff ballet as an "exquisitely plastic instrument for a choreographer to play upon . . . whether the demand upon muscular control seems almost inordinate, as in certain movements of the *Life of the Bee* or the necessity is for such subtle mental feats as memorizing the space and its rhythmic counterpart for *Water Study*."

But it should be noted that Doris Humphrey did not use the human body in an abstract manner. She did not imitate or repeat or create a mechanical pattern in space with human bodies. Although she did not arouse feeling by the romantic method of evoking personal sentiment nor by commanding some bold apparition of grotesque or macabre fantasy, she was concerned with illumination, with an understanding of life, not with decoration, that superficial device to fashion a substitute for living.

Doris Humphrey's people belonged to no class and to no caste. They had human warmth but they did not express a personal emotion. "They give you nothing of their private lives and beliefs as do, for example, the bitter or desolate women of Martha Graham and the small-town dynasts of Charles Weidman."

John Martin said that the greatest danger which beset Doris Humphrey derived from her quality of being able to scale tremendous heights of heroic and noble feeling. Striving to achieve indefinite beauty, she risked being "pretty."

In 1930 the Dance Repertory Theatre was organized by Humphrey, Weidman, Graham and Tamiris. Louis Horst was musical director.

The works created by Doris Humphrey for the Dance Repertory Theatre in 1930-31 included:

Drama of Motion, a long abstract group composition danced in total silence.

The Shakers.

Salutation to the Depths, a duet (Humphrey-Weidman).

Descent into a Dangerous Place, a whimsical solo.

La Valse, to the music of Ravel. A group dance later given with an orchestra.

Dances of Women, a symbolic abstraction of birth and death.

Lake at Evening and *Night Winds,* both lyric solos.

The Call
Breath of Fire } Solos (Humphrey).

Although three of these seven works were solos, one a duet, and two described as "abstract" and symbolic, none was in the pure romantic style, that confidential communication of strictly personal sentiment so dear to Isadora Duncan and Martha Graham.

Doris Humphrey was concerned with reflecting some experience of her own, to be sure, but always in relationship to the outside world. To quote from her declaration:

"I wish my dance to be based on reality illumined by imagination; to be organic rather than synthetic; to call forth a definite reaction from my audience; and to make its contribution toward the drama of life."

Her choreography for Broadway displayed a tremendous variety in form, technique, and an ability to collaborate with an artist of the first rank. She and Charles Weidman made history in their dances and ballet for Molière's *School for Husbands.*

In 1933-34, after creating *Dionysiaques,* a primitive and pagan work about the Sacrifice of the Virgin, and a solo entitled *Two Ecstatic Themes,* Miss Humphrey composed dances for various Broadway revues and theatrical productions, including *Americana,* produced by Lee Shubert, *Run Li'l Chillun,* and Molière's *School for Husbands,* produced by the Theatre Guild.

The Dance: à la Molière, by John Martin, *New York Times,* February 3, 1933:

"Since a ballet forms the entire second act of *School for Husbands* as produced by the Theatre Guild, and since it and the several other incidental dances are choreographed and actually performed by Doris Humphrey and Charles Weidman, the production becomes automatically a subject for the attention of the dance department. . . . The gist of this report is that whatever the production possesses of the style of Molière and the French Theatre of the 17th Century, is due to the labors of Miss Humphrey and Mr. Weidman. Certain exceptions . . . the music arranged by Edmund W. Rickett, Lee Simonson's back drop and some of his costumes, a little scene in the last act in which the Magistrate and the Notary, though somewhat Gilbertian, play at least lustily and farcically.

"In the current issue of the Theatre Arts Monthly, Benedetto Croce has an enlightening article on the Commedia dell' Arte, which is just to the point of the present discussion. '*In Molière,*' he says, '*and in him alone, there live the flowerings of inventions and fantasy of the Italian Commedia dell' Arte. . . .*' Of the Commedia itself, which achieves unification and finish in Molière, Croce writes: 'Buffoonery as they were, *these performances did not have their vital nucleus in poetry or in literature, but in plastic expression and in mimicry.*'"

Molière came to grief in our theatre, John Martin said,

". . . because the style of his theatre has been submerged; the plastic expression, the mimicry (the aching, in other words) have been stifled by the pompous recitation of the *words,* which should really serve only as a useful and charming accompaniment.

"More power, then, to the Theatre Guild, that for once the spell has been partly broken and that in the ballet of Miss Humphrey and Mr. Weidman, we are allowed to see, as through a knothole in a wall, something of the spirit of Molière's theatre.

Miss Humphrey is as captivating and as decorative as the great Isabella herself (Isabella is the heroine of *School for Husbands);* and there is more Molière in one move and gesture of Charles Weidman than in hours of spoken verse.

"Miss Humphrey has done admirable research in composing her dances. She has found the flavor as well as the form of the musettes, minuets and pavanes, and has presented them with such modernizations and adaptations as are necessary to bring them into the tempo of the present theatre.

"The play itself was first produced in 1661, the year in which Louis XIV established the Academy of Music and Dance with his court ballet master, Beauchamp, as director. The interpolated ballet was not done until three years later, but to all intents and purposes, they are contemporaneous. Toe dancing was as yet unknown, the five positions had only just been formulated by Beauchamp, and dancing was largely practiced by the ladies and gentlemen of the court. If there is any criticism justifiable of Miss Humphrey's dancing, it is that she is using a technique that is a little later in date than it might be and the first extant recording of the five positions, in Rameau's *Dancing Master,* published in 1725, shows them to have been even then far less turned out than Miss Humphrey makes them, but this is a quibble. An excellent job has been charmingly done, and one more step taken toward restoring the theatre to its full estate."

For *American,* a Broadway revue produced by Lee Shubert and directed by J. P. McEvoy, Doris Humphrey revived a composition created in 1928, entitled *The Dance of the Chosen.* Based on the theory of dancing one's sins away, *Dance of the Chosen* was re-named *The Shakers.* Program note:

"God hath revealed that eternal life shall be the reward of the chosen few who are shaken clean of sin."* The dance represents the Shaker sect at meeting and is a study of religious ecstasy. The voice, drum and accordion accompaniment were arranged for the dance after it had been created. "It is the first dance of its kind to be based on an American religious theme."

It is worth noting that this work contained some of the most violent, rebellious and mad movement Doris Humphrey created. It was altogether the opposite of her usually exquisite, flowing style, or delicate satirical pantomime. It interpreted the emotions of an Anglo-Saxon religious sect, of a group of men and women dedicated to the principles of celibacy and communism and to the dual character of God (God is man and woman) with the same

* From an old Shaker journal.

mad fury other so-called "modern" dancers used in developing and demonstrating themes of social consciousness.

Miss Humphrey's fine sense of humor may have been suggesting that social consciousness expressed by violent movement is an unconscious revelation of emotional ecstasies neglected by American education and the religion of John Calvin.

At all events, Doris Humphrey's dance was concerned with man, the human being, and his relation to his fellowmen. The problems of class and cult and hierarchy were of secondary interest. She was too feminine to use the percussive Puritan attack of Martha Graham, and too much of a classicist to stomach the Platonic transcendentalism of Ruth St. Denis, or to translate Christian symbols into Indian ideology. As she developed, her compositions became less and less romantic in theme, form and expression, more and more austere and in the great tradition of the classic Greek tragedy.

In 1932, Doris Humphrey became Mrs. Charles F. Woodford. In 1933, Charles Humphrey Woodford was born. In 1934 and each summer thereafter, she and Charles Weidman were artist-faculty members of the Bennington School of the Dance, in Vermont, where Miss Humphrey's trilogy, *New Dance, Theatre Piece,* and *With My Red Fires* had their premières in the summers of 1935 and 1936.

Doris Humphrey wrote:

"During the recent insurgence of art as conflict, I felt that much of the work produced was completely negative and that some affirmation should be made. My trilogy, composed of *New Dance, With My Red Fires,* and *Theatre Piece,* was conceived under such circumstances as these. In the face of a dance world largely proclaiming, 'This is not!,' I would say, 'This is!'

"The first work, *New Dance,* was concerned with social relationships, with a modern brotherhood of man. Since I was conveying an idea and not a concrete program, I built the dance in symphonic form. When it was done, I found a preliminary dance must be composed to show the world as it is today. This work, *Theatre Piece,* gave added force to *New Dance,* which showed the world as it should be.

"Both of these dances were concerned with large social relationships, and I felt that the picture would not be complete without showing something of the relationship of man and woman within this social scheme. In such a way *With My Red Fires* was composed, using both the abstract movement of the first dance and the dramatic movement of the second.

"Each of these dances was planned as to form before it was begun, but how was the first move determined? From the idea . . .

"For instance, in the first part of the *New Dance* the theme required a disconnected, unorganized outpouring of desire from a fragment of a group by the remainder of the group. For this, Charles Weidman and I obviously were the central figures broken off from the group, the rest of the dancers, the onlookers. These two sometimes moved together harmoniously, sometimes at variance, but always restlessly as though in search of a new life. This was the mood of discovery which I needed. The setting for the *New Dance* also came from the idea. I needed blocks at the beginning to suggest an arena from which a crowd looks down. These were used later, piled in the center, to emphasize unity, and balanced harmony achieved at the end. The music was especially composed by Wallingford Riegger."

New Dance, which represented the growth of the individual in relation to his fellows, was not a manifesto of class consciousness. It was revolutionary enough to concern itself with classic man, to accept classic form, to subordinate development and accessory to theme. Had Miss Humphrey chosen to put words in the mouth of her chorus leader, she would have been the American counterpart of a Greek dramatist. As it was, she succeeded in creating a more powerful drama and one of far deeper understanding of the American people than T. S. Eliot and his followers in the literary profession, whose class consciousness and court manners froze their language and their intellects.

Murder in the Cathedral, a paean to Tudor isolationism, was moving to read, hollow and dull to see, impossible to feel.

The best comment on *Theatre Piece,* applauded by critics the country round, was written by John Martin after its performance at the Guild Theatre in New York, February, 1936:

"In a vein of vigorous satire and of nightmarish fantasy, *Theatre Piece* pictures the madness of the competitive system under which we are living. The mysterious under-cover contests and manipulations of business, the pursuit of the eligible husband, the rivalries of the sports arena and of the theatre, all culminate in a relentless race in which groups of contestants march forward over a barrier like so many Golems, and back again with the mechanical futility of a treadmill.

"This is engrossing subject matter in itself, and much of it is engagingly treated. Its finest values, however, are revealed not by the episodes themselves so much as by the presence of an alien figure of protest through whose eyes they are seen. Against the brittle travesty of the group, she moves in a style of complete sincerity and simplicity, a poignant Cassandra-like figure, now struggling to make herself felt, now reduced to tragic and eloquent impotence as she attempts to turn the routine from its reckless patterns to something with meaning and common purpose.

"Though her defeat is inevitably foreshadowed, and by the end of *Theatre Piece* is actually achieved, the second part of the work [the original *New Dance*] presents the ultimate victory of her prophecy. Here we see developed in full and beautiful terms the themes which have been still-born in the earlier section, and the whole work ends with the thrilling *Variations,* in which each individual finds his place in the total pattern with the active support of all the other individuals. Here is propaganda if you will, in its best and fullest sense, not forgetting the consideration of 'social content'; and here is also very fine art."

The third part of the trilogy, *With My Red Fires,* received its title from William Blake's *Jerusalem II:*

"For the Divine Appearance is Brotherhood, but I am Love Elevate into the Region of Brotherhood with my red fires."

With My Red Fires was in two parts performed without break. The characters were: Your Woman, Young Man, and Matriarch.

Part I. "Ritual," composed of three episodes:
1. Hymn to Priapus, danced by Young Man, Young Woman and Group.
2. Search and Betrothal, danced by Young Man, Young Woman and Group.
3. Departure, danced by the same.

Part II. "Drama," in five episodes or scenes:
1. Summons, danced by the Matriarch.
2. Coercion and Escape, danced by the Matriarch and the Young Woman.
3. Alarm, danced by the Matriarch and Group.
4. Pursuit, danced by the Group of Young Men.
5. Judgment, danced by the Young Man, the Young Woman and Group.

Synopsis of action, written for the program notes by Paul Love:

"Hymn to Priapus: The dance opens with a group movement of desire and the longing for completion. The action represents a primitive love-ritual.

"*Search and Betrothal:* Out of this group come the two lovers. Their movements weave in and out of the larger group movements.

"*Departure:* As the departing group comes in contact with the lovers, its movements seem to be majestically changed. You see the group through the lovers' eyes as something new and different.

"*Drama: Summons:* The second part of the dance introduces the Matriarch, who represents a repressive force in society. She is jealous of anyone but herself dominating the girl. She summons the two lovers. Subconsciously the girl feels the magnetic influence of the Matriarch and is drawn to her.

"*Coercion and Escape:* The girl is hypnotized by this influence and, finally submerged by this psychological compulsion, disappears into the house of the Matriarch. The loss of her lover, however, overcomes this malignant power and she returns to him and they escape.

"*Alarm: Pursuit:* This is an affront against society. The Matriarch raises the alarm. She gathers the group, molds it to her opinion, and sends it in pursuit.

"*Judgment:* The lovers are apprehended and driven out by the group. The Matriarch pronounces her judgment upon them. The group, now cold and impersonal, also pronounces judgment. The lovers are left alone, defeated. There is only a brief indication at the end that although cursed by society, the spirit that bound them has not been destroyed."

John Martin, in *The New York Times,* wrote:

"What an unforgettable experience it would be to see the entire *New Dance* trilogy, of which this constitutes a second member, performed on a single program. . . . If it would make for a long evening, certainly the magnitude of the theme of universal brotherhood and the exciting beauty with which it has been translated into choreography, would keep an audience spell-bound to the end. That it would tax a company of dancers terrifically, is not to be denied, but scarcely more than the arduous class and rehearsal sessions to which they regularly subject themselves. Here is an idea for the Federal Theatre to give serious consideration to, for it is manifestly part of its function to sponsor artistic enterprises which are outside the capacity of private individuals.

"From the first phrases of *With My Red Fires,* with the tentative, darting entrances of the dancers in their mystical processional, an uncanny dramatic suspense is established, and with the aid of Wallingford Riegger's admirable music, it is sustained through variation of mood and attack until the final eloquent moment when the two young lovers are at last victoriously together, with a new depth and maturity in their relationship after their persecution.

"*In her creation of the figure of the Matriarch, Doris Hum-*

phrey has evolved a remarkable style to complement the eerie power of the group. It is grotesque almost to the point of being laughable, yet intensely bitter and venomous—tragic; indeed, in the broad sense of the word. Within this convention the character ranges widely from tears and simpering and cajolery by which to win her daughter's obedience to a towering passion which lifts her literally off the ground. There is never a false move or a wasted gesture.

"In the transition from the abstraction of the opening section to the specific miming of the second section, there is no breach of style whatever. The two parts flow together with complete logic, and the final section succeeds in bringing the two manners together into a synthesis that is both beautiful, in an abstract sense, and dramatically exciting."

The compositions that followed the trilogy and which the Humphrey-Weidman group danced on their tours across and around the United States in 1937 were:

To the Dance, a gay opening dance that won the *Dance* Magazine prize award of the year.

American Holiday, a celebration of the death of the hero for the cause of freedom and justice, accompanied by choral singing and the spoken word.

Race of Life, an uproarious satire suggested by the drawings of James Thurber, "might be considered low comedy if performed by any other than Miss Humphrey."

Passacaglia in C Minor (Bach). Miss Humphrey considered this her most mature work.

In 1939 she composed *Square Dances,* a modern interpretation of a square dance followed by four duets with a repetition of the square dance after each duet. The duets were based on four traditional dance forms: country dance, tango, schottische and waltz.

In 1940, the Humphrey-Weidman group moved into a new studio-theatre in New York. *Song of the West* and *Decade* were composed in 1941.

Song of the West was divided into three parts:

1. The Green Land . . . a solo showing the response of the human being to the sunlight and growing things of the earth.

2. Desert Gods . . . group dance beginning with dancers rising from the earth, building up from a processional into a swiftly moving group, with cross-fire pattern; then to circu-

lar, ceremonial pattern with sacrifice at an altar, the figure carried back into the homes of the celebrants, worship and dispersal.

3. Rivers . . . Broad rivers rush to pour themselves into the sea.

Decade was a biography of Humphrey-Weidman dancing for ten years. A speaker, "Mr. Business," tells of the adventures of the dancers.

In this work, the use of words and the character of "Mr. Business" suggested that the choric form Miss Humphrey developed so brilliantly in dance and movement was becoming part of spoken drama.

In 1942 she produced four Chorale Preludes, music by J. S. Bach, *Partita No. 5,* and *El Salon Mexico,* music by Aaron Copland.

In 1944 she composed *Canonade,* music by Paul Nordoff, and *Inquest,* which to the writer's mind is her greatest work and one of the greatest works by any American choreographer.

The theme of *Inquest* is human love—the love that will sacrifice health, the necessities of life, and finally life itself rather than be separated from its humankind; the love that denies the power of the material world, that refuses the benefits of the temporal state of society, that seeks neither heaven on earth nor the pursuit of happiness; the love that rebukes the pride of Platonic and Socratic intellectuals and their scientific rationalism and the urbane discipline of Epicurus who preaches self-restraint the better to enjoy self-indulgence; the love that passes the understanding of the avaricious rich and the envious poor, the love of a man and a woman and a child for one another.

This theme, which is essentially that of St. Thomas Aquinas and the Christian Church, was presented by Doris Humphrey in a modified form of the Greek play.

The story is related by a Narrator who is a modification of the Chorus Leader. The Chorus is represented by a group of dancers described as "People of the Town." The Protagonist is the Collins family—Michael, Mary and their son Cornelius. The Antagonist is the unseen power of organized society, the State, the Master and Tyrant of the Temporal World.

The action is developed by the miming and movement of the Collins family as distinct from the people of the town. The story is brief and simple:

Doris Humphrey in *The Shakers. Dance Collection, New York Public Library at Lincoln Center, Astor, Lenox and Tilden Foundations.*

Charles Weidman as Abe Lincoln. *Dance Collection, New York Public Library at Lincoln Center, Astor, Lenox and Tilden Foundations.*

Martha Graham in *Cave of the Heart. Dance Collection, New York Public Library at Lincoln Center, Astor, Lenox and Tilden Foundations.*

Martha Graham in *Clytemnestra. Martha Swope.*

Eugene Loring and Lew Christensen in *Billy the Kid. Lynes. Dance Collection, New York Public Library at Lincoln Center, Astor, Lenox and Tilden Foundations.*

Ballet from *Oklahoma* with Philip Cook and Claire Pasch. *Van Damm. Dance Collection, New York Public Library at Lincoln Center, Astor, Lenox and Tilden Foundations.*

Agnes de Mille in *Rodeo. Maurice Seymour. Dance Collection, New York Public Library at Lincoln Center, Astor, Lenox and Tilden Foundations.*

West Side Story with Mickey Colin and Lee Becker. *Fred Fehl.*

Gene Kelly in *Pal Joey. Dance Collection, New York Public Library at Lincoln Center, Astor, Lenox and Tilden Foundations.*

Lucia Chase, *Dance Collection, New York Public Library at Lincoln Center, Astor, Lenox and Tilden Foundations.*

George Balanchine. *Martha Swope.*

Jerome Robbins, George Balanchine, and Yuri Gregorivitch. *Victor Alchlomov. Dance Collection, New York Public Library at Lincoln Center, Astor, Lenox and Tilden Foundations.*

Jerome Robbins in *Fancy Free. Alfredo Valente. Dance Collection, New York Public Library at Lincoln Center, Astor, Lenox and Tilden Foundations.*

Lincoln Kirstein. *Martha Swope.*

Michael Collins and his son "translate" boots. It is ill-paid work. The boy loses his eye-sight, the father his health. The mother can not find any purchaser for the mended boots who is able or willing to pay enough to keep the family alive. They are told to go to the poor-house for the hard winter months. But they prefer to stay together. The father dies. Mary Collins lifts up her hands in angry denunciation of the unseen tyrant and the organized society that did not help; but unable to deny her love, she returns to accept the consequences of her choice . . . to be a woman is to suffer the ills of man. The people of the town surround her and her son holds her broken body in his arms.

The musical accompaniment of *Inquest,* written by Norman Lloyd, was supplemented by the sounds of tramping feet, of hammering, of the Narrator's words, of a singer's voice. The effect was one of awesome and troubled lament.

The visual effect was pure drama. Miss Humphrey commanded the vision of the great painters of the Flemish School whose Descents from the Cross were to be seen in the cathedrals of northern Europe.

There was nothing soft or sentimental about *Inquest.* It was not feminine, it was not a plea for more and better public works projects, it was not a Sunday School tract. Above all, it was not sociology.

It was a grave and clear-eyed measure of human life, a measure no one has bothered much about applying since the triumph of Cartesian philosophy and the astounding powers of science as manifested in its conquests of the physical world.

The price of this triumph and its conquests has been man. The mind has killed the heart. There has been some feeble effort made to revive the heart. Sociology, we have thought, might make it beat again. But sociology has done little but make materialism a public concern. It has not said that human beings are not perfectible, that progress is a myth, science nothing but method, and security a matter of faith, not property. The brotherhood of man is no paper plan. It must be fought for. It is necessary to feel love and to prove that feeling in more than words. It is necessary to prove it by some conscious, forceful act. *Inquest* has demonstrated that feeling and proved it.

HUMPHREY'S DANCE TECHNIQUE

Principles of movement
1. *Movement basically a matter of equilibrium or balance.* "My entire technique consists of the development of the process of falling away from and returning to equilibrium."
2. *Emotional implications.* "Exciting danger of the fall, and the repose and peace of the recovery."

Extension of movement into studies
"To dance well, technical mastery of the body is the first prerequisite. And since my dance grows out of natural bodily movement, training for it must involve natural movements."

1. *Body mechanics*
   a. *Stretches* . . . to give body strength, flexibility, endurance and coördination. Body bends; special exercises for feet, knee, thighs, legs, torso, etc.
   b. *Walks, runs, jumps and leaps* . . . fundamental natural movements.

2. *Dance studies*
   a. *First series of falls* . . . simple complete falls and recoveries in four directions. Give balance and control in all body positions.
   b. *Second series of falls* . . . more elaborate and difficult, involving preparatory movements.
   c. *Design studies.*
   d. *Studies in contrasts of design and dynamics.*
   e. *Variations* . . . combinations of all elements with stress on rhythms and many more, numbering at least thirty.

Doris Humphrey retired as a performer in 1945 and for the rest of her life dedicated herself to choreographing for and guiding the José Limón troupe. The important works of this period were *Day on Earth, Ritmo Jondo, Night Spell, Ruins and Visions, Invention, Theater Piece No. 2,* and *Brandenburg Concerto No. 4.*

In 1955, with the help of Martha Hill, director of dance at the Juilliard School of Music, Miss Humphrey founded the Juilliard Dance Theater. *The Art of Making Dances,* a major book on choreography, was published posthumously in 1959 by Rinehart, New York.

CHAPTER VI

CHARLES WEIDMAN

MINSTREL SLAYS GOLIATH

The revolt of Isadora Duncan launched a great Romantic Movement. The repressive order of John Calvin, the middle-class imperialism of Victoria, and the insufferable elegance of ponderous Edwardian etiquette, no longer went unchallenged. They had to meet a succession of challengers, various personifications of the individual man who did not acquiesce to the social system they imposed. Isadora Duncan invoked the Spirit of Joy to banish the bleak ghouls of Militant Puritanism. Ted Shawn recalled Hercules to kill Medusa; Ruth St. Denis dared say that Christian woman was a sensual creature, and Martha Graham, that lust had made her a violent one. Doris Humphrey left Olympian heights and discovered that compassion alone had sufficient power to civilize man. But none of these great artists had concerned themselves about the social system that was actually replacing the one they condemned.

Charles Weidman was the first American choreographer to turn aside from the subject of Man, the individual, free and dedicated to "Progress," and to choose as his theme that design of which man is a part—Society. Charles Weidman, satirist, was defining the character of our society as Molière and Beaumarchais did in seventeenth and eighteenth century France.

After his period of apprenticeship as a student, first of Eleanor Frampton in his home town, Lincoln, Nebraska, then of Ruth St. Denis, Ted Shawn and Doris Humphrey in the classes and productions of the Denishawn School, Charles Weidman helped Doris Humphrey found a school in 1927, shortly after the return of the Denishawn troupe from the Orient.

Not long after founding the school, Doris Humphrey and Charles Weidman, experimenting with a new technique and devoting themselves particularly to American themes, performed

97

with a company of their own in New York and at colleges and university theatres throughout the country.

Although Weidman's independent work was very much part of Doris Humphrey's, the dancers were complementary to one another, never in competition nor in conflict. Weidman was a satirist who worked in the medium of pantomime. Humphrey's idealism took the form of classic tragedy. The difference between them might be compared to the difference between Molière and Racine.

Our minstrel show, modified, became Weidman's so-called "kinetic pantomime." This phrase, coined by John Martin and which was also the title of a dance by Weidman, described the application of the rhythm characteristic of our people to the gesture which is an expression of their feeling.

Weidman applied himself to intensifying the rhythmic design of our life. His apprenticeship over, he composed the excellent American pantomime of manners, *Daddy Was a Fireman.* Before making a detailed analysis of this work, a survey of his early compositions will be useful and advisable.

Paul Love, in an article about Charles Weidman published in 1934 in the *Dance Observer,* remarked that despite Charles Weidman's fitness for comedy and burlesque, "or because of it, he was temporarily lost in the God-Complex."

The natural bent toward pantomime persisted, however, and Weidman became famous the country around for *Danse Américaine* in 1923. *Dance Lovers* Magazine, in June, 1925, published the following article about *Danse Américaine:*

"One of the first real American dances we have ever seen was Charles Weidman's *Danse Américaine,* presented in the Denishawn program. There was something about it so different, so clever and so catchy that it seemed you must see it over and over again until you grasped every detail. Then you want to go home and try its popular sport steps yourself."

The following article was written by Charles Weidman:

DANSE AMÉRICAINE
Created by Mr. Shawn and Danced by Charles Weidman
of Denishawn

"This dance is purely pantomime, which is the most important thing to remember throughout. Pantomime is, as a rule, a gift. Some dance students never become proficient in that art, others find it comes to them naturally. Pantomime is one of the greatest aids to moving-picture actors and actresses, and one of the main reasons for the many failures in the pictures is due to the lack of this natural art.

"Every dancer should try to perfect his pantomime. It is not so necessary in ballet work, but for character dances and Oriental interpretations it is absolutely essential. If you are not good in pantomime, if you fail, as a rule, to put it over, you will find practicing this little dance will help you a great deal.

"The costuming is important. You must put your audience in the spirit of the dance from the moment you appear on the stage, and the only way to get this effect is to have. music and costume absolutely suitable. . . . The suit is tight-fitting and small; a vivid shade of tan is the most effective color. The shoes are the 'bulldog' type, of the color known as 'yellow' tan. Light socks, striped shirt, bright tie and a derby complete the ensemble.

"The character is a small mill-town 'dude.' He is the sport of the town and knows it! He is afraid of nothing on earth—but the 'skoits'! Remember to keep this spirit of bravado throughout the entire dance.

"The dance itself can be done without knowledge of technique. There are no regular fixed steps to it; it is merely the interpretation of a story, by gestures, to suitable music.

"As you walk on the stage you are supposed to be coming down the street, all dressed up in your best clothes, with an eye open to everyone's envious glance, your hands in your pockets, chest thrown out and a real swagger. Over to the right you see a friend. You motion to him with your hand, and at the same moment you see another friend over to the other side. In a few minutes you are the center of an admiring imaginary circle, and parade about, showing off your new outfit!

"Presently you suggest a game of craps. You stand still, leaning forward, hands on your hips, watching your imaginary chums try their luck. Then with a scornful gesture you place your hat on the ground, kneel down, and generally prepare for action! After much coaxing and shaking of the bones, you 'roll 'em out' and find that you have won everything.

"More pleased with yourself than ever, you walk over to where a game of baseball is in progress. Your offer to pitch awhile is accepted. But you soon tire of this and ask for a chance to bat. You put your hat down for a base and after two strikes you line out one which you think is going to be a home run. However, the umpire calls you 'out' after a slide for third base, and after telling him your opinion of his judgment and threatening to 'knock him for a row of ash-cans,' you walk away in search of new fields to conquer.

"Then you meet a beautiful girl, but fear of her is uppermost, and you start to walk away. She smiles encouragingly and, conquering your embarrassment, you ask her to come to the dance with you. To your great delight, she accepts. You take your imaginary partner in your arms and dance for a moment, but your bliss is shattered by a collision with another couple. You are belligerent and start to fight, but remembering you have a lady with you, you gallantly take her by the arm and lead her away.

"She is very proud of you and her praises gradually go to your head. You tell her she hasn't seen anything yet and start to dance for her. This can be any type with which you are most familiar, tap, clog, soft shoe, etc. If you prefer, you may put in a few amusing eccentric steps.

"You are very pleased with the applause you receive and walk off the stage, completely forgetting your partner. . . . As the applause dies down, you notice your girl. Full of apologies, you take her arm and lead her off the stage with you, making explanations as you go.

"Never lose your character in the pantomime, and put over each idea as clearly as possible. It is not an artistic dance but in the usual recital program is a welcome novelty."*

The building of pantomime in dance form produced *Minstrels,* a composition for a small group. In *The Ringside,* a dance for two men, Weidman correlated narrative and form so closely that the movements of the fight became a dance.

Miss St. Denis described the Denishawn student of a year as one whose deftness and humor always enchanted her. "He was superb in the Crap-shooter Ted had created for him, and whenever his poignant, wistful *Pierrot†* was on the program, I never failed to creep out front to see it." Strength, that fetish of pioneer countries, was replaced by style. It was impossible not to sense the subtle rebuke Charles Weidman made in all his dance and pantomime to bigness as such. He ridiculed without malice, but also without mercy, brawn and muscle admired for their own sake. (Was this a practical way of reminding Americans that a magnificent industrial equipment does not guarantee a fine way of life?)

---

* *Dance Lovers* Magazine, June, 1925.
† *Pierrot,* inspired by the poem, *Pierrot Sings* by Harold Vinal.

Marionette Show, in 1929, was followed by *The Happy Hypocrite,* first produced in 1931, then in its re-worked and expanded form in 1932.

From Crap-shooter, to Pierrot, to Minstrel, to Prize-fighter, to Wicked Sir George Hell . . . Charles Weidman had experience in many societies: the realistic, swaggering street, the wistful retreat of dreams, the land of the strolling troubadour, the battleground of sport and the dissipated luxury of titled aristocracy. He learned the gestures of these societies and distorted them into a pattern. In 1933, he attempted a dance and pantomime version of that masterpiece of philosophical satire, Voltaire's *Candide.*

But the two-hour-long pantomime *Candide* was not as successful a composition as *The Happy Hypocrite.* Max Beerbohm's tale of the Restoration style roué who dupes innocent Jenny Mere by holding a mask before his wicked face, only to be reformed by the innocent Jenny, can be well and wittily told in a pantomime dance of three scenes, but the story of the adventures of a gullible rustic who believes in the promises of plutocrats, was not successfully told by recitation from a great gilt mask of Voltaire set up alongside the proscenium accompanying the action on the stage.

But as an experiment, this production was useful preparation for the later and better combining of words and dance in *Daddy Was a Fireman,* and the gradual return to the Greek form of theatre.

After *Candide* came what Paul Love describes as a "theatre interlude." Charles Weidman had several important roles in Theatre Guild and other Broadway productions, and did dances for the New York Repertory Company. In the fall of 1933, he did a "cotillon" for Joe Cook's *Hold Your Horses* and three dances for *As Thousands Cheer.* The last three were described as being much more than theatre pieces, as material that belonged in Mr. Weidman's recital repertoire, particularly the numbers entitled *The Lonely Heart's Column* and *Revolt in Cuba.*

In 1934, at Bennington, Vermont, when the summer school of the dance was inaugurated, Charles Weidman was engaged as a staff teacher. The importance of this connection was two-fold.

First, as a theatre for his serious compositions; second, as the source of a new and stimulating audience. In 1935, Bennington witnessed *American Saga,* a dance work by Charles Weidman and his male group, which had had an earlier performance at the Park Theatre in New York (May 3 and 4, 1935) under the auspices of the New Dance League and the Dance Theatre. The program had announced that the sponsors dedicated themselves to combatting War, Fascism, and Censorship; and on the same bill was another Weidman composition, *Tradations,* a work "salted with pantomime humor."

Frederick Allen King, editor of the *Literary Digest,* noted, as surprising, that the "obviously proletarian audience" at the Park Theatre demanded the only encore of the evening from William Dollar, "whose fluent grace in a variation devised by George Balanchine, brought forth loud applause."

But why should *American Saga,* dealing as it did with the career of Paul Bunyan, interest an audience of recently transplanted Europeans, whose culture was primarily neither Norse nor Anglo-Saxon? Although José Limón danced the part of Paul Bunyan, the theme was still the power of physical strength.

In Bennington, however, visitors came from practically every state, even from as far as Honolulu. *American Saga* was repeated with more success, and in 1936 *Quest* had its première at the summer school. *Quest* was a major work. Danced to the music of Norman Lloyd, its main theme concerned the role of the artist in our society. Weidman expressed his belief that the artist was the true spokesman of mankind. Shawn's pre-occupation with art as religion, in the substitution of dances for the hierarchy of a priesthood, had no place at all in Weidman's philosophy. To his mind, Art as a cult and artists in ivory towers would languish or be unknown. The argument of *Quest* was stated in the terms of the artist's struggle "to discover or to create conditions under which he may achieve full and free expression. The artist must be part of society. He encounters many obstacles, in many lands. Today he struggles alone with nothing but his inner strength to aid him. Perhaps tomorrow he will unite his forces with those of his fellows and reach his goal."

In the performance of *Quest,* two levels were used for the action. On the lower level, the artist, played by Charles Weidman, slowly emerges from the crowd. On the upper level, his Inspiration, played by Doris Humphrey, follows his course. His first works are attacked by the critics. They disagree among themselves and the public rejects the artist. In an effort to save himself, he seeks patronage among the women, but they degrade him to the state of a gigolo. He flees from them in an interlude danced by men, and is next reincarnated in contemporary Germany, where he is classified according to racial and political ideas, only to be thrown to the dogs of war under the insignia of "Pro Patria." The allegorical figure finally emerges to inspire new "affirmations," and the crowd unites to face the future with a common purpose.

This work was very similar in feeling to what Victor Hugo expressed in his ode entitled *Le Poete,* a poem written for a collection of lyrics composed between 1819 and 1827.

The ode is dedicated to Lamartine, whose apostrophe "Muse, contemplate thy victim!" is inscribed under the title of the ode. Charles Weidman, like Victor Hugo, seemed to have had some trouble reconciling the pagan "must" and the Christian morality.

Frederick Allen King's comment about *Quest* was:

"Certain aspects . . . inevitably suggest such predecessors as the Swedish and the Jooss ballets. Also, it seems a mistake to localize any of the episodes in any particular country."

With *Quest,* Charles Weidman seemed to have ended his apprenticeship. Allegory and fantasy no longer occupied him. He began to study the life of the people around him.

Then came *This Passion,* a dance based on three themes which include an air raid and the tragedy of the Snyder-Gray murder case; *Opus 51,* our every-day life from vacuum cleaning to camp meeting. in a design of stylized pantomime; *Flickers,* a satire on the silent cinema.

On My Mother's Side, a gently satirical dig at pioneer genealogy (almost a Mid-west Burke's peerage), preceded *Daddy Was a Fireman* and bore out the promise of the statement Charles Weidman wrote for the folder describing the Humphrey-Weidman Dance Group and Theatre:

" 'Modern'—what does this word mean? The dictionary defines it as 'pertaining to the present time,' but it is not enough to be merely existing in the contemporary world. Active life demands that we be mentally and emotionally aware of the world's continual chance and realize the constant progressions and retrogressions.

"The artist who attempts to escape the present, either by delving into the past or the future, is running away from his 'center of being.' But it is not enough for the artist alone to assume his responsibilities *as mentor and preceptor*. His audience also must do so, especially in the case of an artistic form which concerns the theatre.

"The concert dance lives only while it is being presented. It cannot be referred to later in files or books. Therefore, both *the stage and the auditorium have equal importance. Those who sit in the 'house' must also be of today. They also must be conscious of and sensitive to their age, for only then will the dance work come alive and project its true meaning and value as the artist wished.*

"Modernism in the dance requires that we, both artist and audience, be not blind to the life that surrounds us, nor shut ourselves off from it into fantasy and romance. It demands that we be part of it and merge with it. It calls upon us, as artists, to become mouthpieces for its expression; to cease being static and self-satisfied; to be ready each year to say new things and to say them in new ways; to keep our mode of expression fresh and vital; and to remove the dance from pleasant entertainment that lulls us into vague nostalgia, to a strong living art that touches us powerfully as we are today."

In this piece of writing, Charles Weidman said exactly the same thing Louis Jouvet said in his *Réflexions du Comédien*—advice to the audiences of the European and American theatre that without the active collaboration of poet, actor and audience there may be a spectacle or a lecture . . . but never a play.

The theme of *Daddy Was a Fireman* is the war between the Greeks and the Amazons. Its form is that of a danced play; the time, that moment when a pioneer civilization has come to an end; the place, Lincoln, Nebraska.

The Protagonist must triumph within the boundaries of organized society; his feats of prowess must be in behalf of conventions and established forms of living, not an exhibition of daring, of adventuresome combat against "Indians," of the conquest of the physical properties of another people.

He becomes the servant of the state—Fire Commissioner. He marries—not one of the hustling, energetic local Amazons, but a visiting belle from Sioux City. She reigns as first lady of the town because she is wife to the Chief. The Amazons are transformed into clubwomen and commiserate with the Chief's wife when she is left at home by order of the Governor of the State, who promotes the Fire Commissioner of Lincoln, Nebraska, to command the Fire Departments of the Canal Zone.

In the production of *Daddy Was a Fireman* at the Humphrey-Weidman Theatre, in 1943 and 1944, the Protagonist was played by Charles Weidman, the Visiting Belle by Doris Humphrey, and "Fire," symbol of Public Enemy No. 1, was danced by Peter Hamilton.

A chorus of women spoke, danced and acted; a small group recited the prologue and comments about the action of the principal characters.

Charles Weidman was born on July 22, 1901, in Lincoln, Nebraska, the son of Charles Edward and Vesta Hoffman Weidman. His father was fire chief of the Canal Zone at the time the Panama Canal was being built. His mother was champion roller-skater of the Middle West. He was talented with the pencil, and his early ambitions were in the direction of cartoons, drawing, and architecture. However, when the Denishawn group played in Lincoln, Nebraska, he became interested in the dance and, from 1919 to 1921, studied with Eleanor Frampton of Lincoln, Nebraska. In 1921, he went to Los Angeles, studying with the Denishawns and with Theodore Koslov. His first opportunity came when the King in *Xochitl* broke his toe and he was asked to take his place. He was an immediate success, and from then on, was featured with the Denishawns. (Martha Graham was being featured as the King's daughter.) In 1928, he formed a school of the dance with Doris Humphrey. He composed *The Happy Hypocrite, Candide,* and *Kinetic Pantomime.*

In summing up Charles Weidman's contribution to the art of theatre and dance in the United States, it is the opinion of the writer that he defined the stock characters of the classic comedy in the contemporary idiom: a cult that had created the Wife as Ornament and Glamour Girl, our worship of classic beauty, our enjoyment of physical comfort which has created a voluptuous and ample matron successor to the Amazon, the urchin boy, the symbol of our uncontrolled nature of a small boy, half satyr, half hooligan, who can fish and also shoot crap, the dandy who will abandon any fashion as soon as it becomes commonplace, who is perhaps the archetype of the American man.

These characters were recognized with delight by the audiences who saw *Daddy Was a Fireman* and *On My Mother's Side*.

The writer would like to repeat the wish often made by those who saw these dance works: "We hope there will be more things like this."

In 1945 Charles Weidman created his own dance school, in 1948 his own dance group and his most famous work, *Fables of Our Time,* based on James Thurber's fables. *The War Between Men and Women,* another Thurber work, was choreographed in 1954.

In the late fifties and thereafter Weidman concentrated on teaching, giving master classes in many colleges in the United States. Some of the outstanding modern dancers of the day have been his pupils.

CHAPTER VII

A BRIEF NOTE ON THE BALLET

Ballet originated in Rome at the time of Augustus Caesar. The miming of Roman buffoons and the acrobatic feats of Etruscan rope dancers and gymnasts were combined by two imaginative and enterprising geniuses of the time, named Pylades and Bathylle.

Pylades taught athletes how to act; Bathylle stylized the leaps, bends, and turns used by the skillful Etruscans and recorded movements which have today become an integral part of what we call classic choreography.

Virtuosity in its crude state became an art. It presently became a method of education, for Pylades made notations of the choreographic and pantomime technique.

Italy, therefore, must be rightly acknowledged the cradle of ballet.

In the reign of Louis XIV, ballet became court or social dancing. The "five positions" were taught to kings, princes and princesses, and the comedies of Molière were embellished by interludes of dancing that emphasized the theme of the play.

But ballet did not stay long at Versailles. It moved to the stage when Lulli started his opera at the Jeu de Paume du Bel Air, and when Noverre, taking up where Pylades had left off, re-united "ballet d'action" or pantomime with what had become, during a stay at court, a technique of pose and movement.

Half a century later, Filippo Taglioni (1778-1871), Italian dancer and choreographer who made his debut at Pisa in 1794 and created *Les Sylphides*, first produced in Paris in 1732, founded the Romantic School of ballet.

He discarded the classic sandal and substituted for it the satin slipper we call "toe shoe." He dismissed the stock scenery that represented temples, palaces and the gods on the mount of Olympus. He dressed his daughter Marie in white gauze, crowned her

107

dark hair with a simple wreath of flowers, gave her a pair of wings, and taught her to dance in the legendary land of elfs, fairies, sprites and sylphs. He robbed her of her human character and made her one of the eternal romantic spirits.

"Toe dancing" revolutionized ballet technique. Camargo had studied only three months before she was engaged at the age of ten as the first dancer at the Brussels Opera House. After Taglioni's revolution, the career of ballerina became a life work.

Two schools of Romantic Ballet, the Italian and the French, competed for the favor of audiences in the opera houses of Europe. The Italian school, more "acrobatic" than "artistic," reproached the French school for its cold, impersonal quality. The French opera ballet had the honor of sending its star to dance at the Scala Opera in Milan. French technique and French style were imitated by Italian ballerinas. But the result was not wholly satisfactory. Italian dancers lost their quality of expression, executed movements correctly but without grace.

What was needed were new composers, new librettists and a new impresario.

In 1830, the Paris Opera was confronted with a million franc deficit. Sosthene de La Rochefoucault's resignation was accepted and he was replaced by Veron, shrewd, self-made and ambitious, whose goal was to make the opera "the Versailles of the new bourgeóis aristocracy" (bankers, brokers, law clerks).

The opera house was renovated; gilt, plush, and crystal chandeliers were installed with lavish profusion. But Veron knew enough to choose such composers as Auber, Meyerbeer, and Adam, and to enlist the talent of Scribe. He was intelligent enough to realize the bourgeois aristocracy wanted a spectacle after dinner, nothing that would interfere with their digestion. His productions of opera anticipated the music hall and the moving picture, were exclusively a feast for the eye. The great ballerinas of the day, Marie Taglioni and Fanny Elssler, each with her own following, advertised Veron's product and attracted impassioned and militant admirers who preached the cult of Taglionism or Elsslerism.

In 1851, Marie and Fanny retired, and the ballet slowly declined again. Imitation followed imitation. Poses and gestures became mechanical. The opera ballet was a piece of stage business, the ballerina a *bourgeoise en tutu*. Who would be the twentieth century renovator? Wherefrom the new life blood of the ballet?

France replied to this question with one word—Stravinsky. The French described him as the only composer since Lulli who knew how to borrow the plastic rhythm of the dance and return it in the form of sound.

Russia's reply was the choreography of Fokine, and Stravinsky, the dancing of Pavlowa, Mordkin, Nijinsky, Nureyev and others.

From the United States the answer is summed up in the careers of Duncan, Shawn, St. Denis, Graham, Humphrey, Weidman, Joffrey, Cunningham, Taylor, Ailey, Feld. Also Balanchine and Robbins.

From England the answer is summed up in the brilliant administration leadership of Marie Rambert and Ninette de Valois, and in the choreography and dancing of Tudor, Alicia Markova and Margot Fonteyn.

In Germany, Mary Wigman inspired generations of dancers in the United States.

CHAPTER VIII

BALLET COMPANIES AFTER 1945
ENTER JEROME ROBBINS
ALMOST OVERNIGHT, A NEW MASTER
IN THE HOUSE

When Lucia Chase and Richard Pleasant created the American Ballet Theatre in 1940, the corps and the soloists were trained according to the high style of classic dance perfected, clarified, and taught by Marius Petipa (1819–1910), Marseilles-born choreographer and dancer of the Imperial Russian Ballet.*

And in 1948 when Lincoln Kirstein and George Balanchine fashioned the New York City Ballet from their American Ballet the same was true about their corps de ballet and soloists. Even moreso perhaps because Balanchine had entered the Imperial School of Ballet (1914—he was ten years old) after Fokine had left to work with Diaghilev in Paris and the school had dropped Fokine's innovations. In Balanchine's words: "I was brought up in St. Petersburg. The style of dancing there was very strict and precise. At the same time in Moscow, six hundred kilometers away, the style of dancing was close to a circus performance. . . . History shows that the dancers and choreographers who later influenced ballet as a whole came mainly from St. Petersburg [Leningrad]."

A recent ballet historian remarks that to this day the ballet in Soviet Russia is largely based on the repertoire of Petipa—productions such as *The Sleeping Beauty, Raymonda, La Bayadère,* and the restaged *Giselle* and *Swan Lake.*

Petipa tradition ruled in both major American ballet com-

* The Imperial Russian Ballet is now renamed the Kirov Ballet.

110

panies until the arrival of a young dancer who had danced in the chorus at Radio City Music Hall. His name was Jerome Robbins, and he was auditioned and accepted as a member of the Ballet Theatre corps in the early forties.

At the first performance of *Three Virgins and a Devil,* a comic ballet by Agnes de Mille, Jerome Robbins in a walk-on part stole the show. No one was prepared for the explosion that followed the premiere of the former walk-on performer's *Fancy Free* on April 18, 1944, at the Metropolitan Opera House on 39th Street. There were twenty curtain calls for the one-acter about three sailors on the town, danced by Robbins, John Kriza, and Hugh Laing, with music by Leonard Bernstein. Edwin Denby, dean of American dance critics, pronounced it "superb super-vaudeville." "Jerome Robbins mates the forward attitudes of classical ballet," wrote James Klosty, "the cakewalk of the minstrel show, the African rhythms of jazz, the acrobatics of modern dance, the chorus line of musical comedy and perhaps most important of all 'mime', *the body language that expresses a personal feeling,* [Winthrop Palmer's italics] that element of theatre dance that Lincoln Kirstein rejects with noble outrage."

How did this happen? How did Robbins stylize local dance dialect such as the trucking, for example, the boogie, knee-drops, and a round-the-back-door in slow motion, and graft it onto the vocabulary of ballet and theatre dancing?

The director of any great school of the dance will shrug his or her shoulders at this question. Any character dancer learns to use "syncopated" accents and to develop muscles not used by the movements of the classic dance. Not all character dancers go to the best schools, however, or are willing to take instruction if they do. There is always the rebel, the improvisor, like so many so-called modern dancers, who are in effect, demi-caractère, caractère, or folk dancers.

In this writer's opinion Jerome Robbins at his best is a reincarnation of the Italian Commèdia's *Harlequin,* of Molière's *Scapin,* and of Beaumarchais's *Figaro.*

What has Robbins said in his thirty-one or so ballets, in the many ballet skits that have added novelty and dimension to conventional music comedies, in musical comedies inspired by a one-act ballet (such as *On the Town* by *Fancy Free*), in a "musical" that he fashioned and directed himself like *Fiddler on the Roof?* And in the multitude of reproductions and imitations by photography and recording of his work. Is there a constant theme in all this superb character dancing, a backbone of social comment? Is there content as well as technique? And if so, what?

The ingenious scamp who scrambled out of the chorus to make star billing, the Harlequin of sorts who can dance, clown, or mime anyone out of countenance anywhere, anytime, and whose one of many titles is Jerome Robbins, like Figaro in the 1780s defends human rights and the common man (milkman, sailor, gangster, and girl) against the elegant and faintly corrupt attitudes of an imperial establishment.

THE ABSTRACT BALLETS OF GEORGE BALANCHINE
AFTER 1945

The genius of George Balanchine is an accepted fact. He has no rival in his particular field, which is classic ballet in the Petipa tradition and its grafting into twentieth-century America.

It is as impossible for George Balanchine to design a cheap ballet or one without style as it would have been for Raphael or Picasso, for that matter, to draw badly.

And yet there is something missing in the pure dance suites set to the music of Stravinsky, and other contemporary composers for the New York City Ballet. The so-called experimental manipulations of classical technique such as *Opus 34, Ivesiana, Agon, Episodes, Electronics,* executed by American dancers whose athletic bodies Balanchine likes to celebrate, have an arid quality. There is an almost absolute lack of lyric poetry.

The American dancers create bold and intricate patterns in space. But for all our temporary tinkering with technology there is much more to America than an aptitude for pure math. "The vocabulary of the filling stations and the grocery stores on the Main Streets of this country is essentially based on a love of sport."

Balanchine dancers do not seem to be animated by the love of anything. Their superbly trained athletic bodies obediently execute graceful or stirring exercises and exhibitions of elegant gymnastics. Much more should be given them to do. Dance that is human as well as an elegant discipline. Dance that is an affirmation of moral courage as well as physical power.

The great Russian choreographer is really more at home and at ease in the restaging of such classics as *Firebird, Swan Lake,*

The Nutcracker, and in making full-length ballets out of such literary masterpieces as *A Midsummer Night's Dream* and *Don Quixote.* His American company dance fairy story and dramatic ballets with conviction and energy in the vast State Theatre auditorium in Lincoln Center that Philip Johnson announced he had designed for George Balanchine and his New York City Ballet.

THE REPERTOIRE OF
NEW YORK CITY BALLET AND AMERICAN BALLET THEATRE

In the 1950s, an audience at the American Ballet Theatre or at the New York City Ballet would see examples of classic dance, character dance, and, at the American Ballet Theatre, of danced pantomimes by Antony Tudor, described by George Balanchine as "tragedies of manner." Each company had its version of *Swan Lake.* Each had its character ballets by Jerome Robbins and its abstract (no story) ballets by George Balanchine.

A typical American Ballet Theatre program of the fifties would present:

Metropolitan Opera House
Broadway between 39th and 40th Streets
Tuesday evening, April 12, 1955

The ballets danced were: *Les Sylphides* by Michel Fokine, music by Frederic Chopin; *Pillar of Fire* by Antony Tudor, music by Arnold Schoenberg; *Pas de Deux* (the Black Swan from *Swan Lake*) choreography after Petipa, music by Tchaikovsky; *Fancy Free* by Jerome Robbins, music by Leonard Bernstein.

A typical New York City Ballet program of the fifties would present:

New York City Center
131 W. 55 Street
Tuesday evening, November 8, 1955

The ballets danced were: *Serenade* by George Balanchine, music by Tchaikovsky; *Age of Anxiety* by Jerome Robbins, music by Leonard Bernstein; *Sylvia: Pas de Deux* by George Balanchine,

Metropolitan Opera House

Broadway between 39th and 40th Streets

TUESDAY EVENING, APRIL 12, 1955

BALLET THEATRE FOUNDATION
BLEVINS DAVIS, President

presents

THE BALLET THEATRE

LUCIA CHASE and OLIVER SMITH, Directors

ALICIA ALONSO   IGOR YOUSKEVITCH   NORA KAYE   JOHN KRIZA
RUTH ANN KOESUN   ERIC BRAUN   LUPE SERRANO
ERIK BRUHN   SONIA AROVA

SCOTT DOUGLAS   BARBARA LLOYD   JOB SANDERS
CATHERINE HORN   FERNAND NAULT   CHRISTINE MAYER
ENRIQUE MARTINEZ   MARIA ANGELICA

and returning as guest artists,
former members of THE BALLET THEATRE dancing in their familiar roles

ALICIA MARKOVA

PATRICIA BOWMAN   ANTON DOLIN   HUGH LAING
MARY ELLEN MOYLAN   TATIANA RIABOUCHINSKA

MURIEL BENTLEY   MARY BURR   VIOLA ESSEN   MARIA KARNILOVA
PAULA LLOYD   ANNABELLE LYON   SONO OSATO   NINA STROGANOV
JENNY WORKMAN
EDWARD CATON   ROY FITZELL   YUREK LAZOWSKY   JAMES MITCHELL
DAVID NILLO   NICOLAS ORLOFF   DONALD SADDLER   SIMON SEMENOFF

and choreographers appearing in their own ballets

AGNES DE MILLE   DAVID LICHINE   ANTONY TUDOR

Musical Director   Regisseur   Guest Conductor
JOSEPH LEVINE   DIMITRI ROMANOFF   DANIEL SAIDENBERG

Management S. HUROK

The Ballet Theatre program. *Copyright PLAYBILL. All rights reserved, used by permission.*

NEW YORK CITY CENTER

of Music and Drama

FIRE NOTICE: The exit indicated by a red light and sign nearest to the seat you occupy is the shortest route to the street. In the event of fire please do not run—WALK TO THAT EXIT.
EDW. F. CAVANAGH, JR.
FIRE COMMISSIONER

Thoughtless persons annoy patrons and distract actors and endanger the safety of others by lighting matches during the performance and intermissions. This violates a city ordinance and renders the offender liable to ARREST. It is urged that all patrons refrain from lighting matches in the auditorium of this theatre.

THIS ✦ PROGRAM ✦ IS ✦ PUBLISHED ✦ BY ✦ PLAYBILL ✦ INCORPORATED

TUESDAY EVENING, NOVEMBER 8; WEDNESDAY EVENING, NOVEMBER 9;
THURSDAY EVENING, NOVEMBER 10, AND FRIDAY EVENING, NOVEMBER 11, 1955

IN THE EVENT OF AN AIR RAID ALARM REMAIN IN YOUR SEATS AND OBEY THE INSTRUCTIONS OF THE MANAGEMENT.—ROBERT E. CONDON, DIRECTOR OF CIVIL DEFENSE.

NEW YORK CITY BALLET

MARIA TALLCHIEF   TANAQUIL LeCLERCQ   DIANA ADAMS

PATRICIA WILDE   MELISSA HAYDEN   YVONNE MOUNSEY   JILLANA

NICHOLAS MAGALLANES   FRANCISCO MONCION   HERBERT BLISS

TODD BOLENDER   ROY TOBIAS   JACQUES D'AMBOISE

and

ANDRE EGLEVSKY

LEON BARZIN, Musical Director

THE NEW YORK CITY BALLET ORCHESTRA

Conductors: LEON BARZIN and HUGO FIORATO

Ballet Mistress: VIDA BROWN

New York City Ballet program. *Copyright PLAYBILL. All rights reserved, used by permission.*

music by Léo Délibes; *Western Symphony* by George Balanchine, music by Hershy Kay.

When the New York City Ballet toured Russia in 1962 its repertoire included fifteen ballets by Balanchine, two by Robbins.

The Robbins ballets were *Games* to music by Morton Gould and *Fanfare* to music by Benjamin Britten. The Balanchine ballets were: *Agon,* music by Stravinsky; *Raymonda,* music by Glazounov; *Allegro Brillante,* music by Tchaikovsky; *Symphony in C,* music by Bizet; *Scotch Symphony,* music by Mendelssohn; *Concerto Barocco,* music by Bach; *Donizetti Variations; La Sonnàmbula,* Rieti after themes by Bellini; *Divertimento #15,* music by Mozart; *Prodigal Son,* music by Prokofiev; *La Valse,* music by Ravel; *Apollo,* music by Stravinsky; *Episodes,* music by Anton Webern; also *Serenade* and *Western Symphony.*

Russian audiences and Russian dance critics liked the work of Jerome Robbins. But some dance critics wrote that Edward Villella, New York City Ballet's premier danseur, was physically better suited to "demi-caractère" than to first dancer roles. True enough. But in the 1960s the American male preferred ball (base, basket, or foot) and the discipline of athletics to that of a ballet school.

From time to time American Ballet Theatre and the New York City Ballet announced new works by promising young choreographers. *Pas des Déesses* by Robert Joffrey was danced by the American Ballet Theatre; George Balanchine encouraged Jacques d'Amboise, a promising first dancer, to choreograph for the company. But no major new talent was discovered this way. Other sponsors, Rebekah Harkness, Alexander Ewing, the YMHA, the Ford Foundation, the City Center and the Federal government helped launch the Joffrey Ballet Company and the Alvin Ailey Dance Theatre, whose repertoires and American-born choreographers found large new audiences from "Maine to California," and on European tours.

CHAPTER IX

NEW COMPANIES
AND
CHOREOGRAPHERS

THE ROBERT JOFFREY BALLET*

The Robert Joffrey Ballet was named for a young choreographer from Seattle, Washington, Robert Joffrey, whose name at birth in 1930 was Abdullah Jaffa Anver Bey Khan. His father was Afghan, his mother Italian.

He studied dancing in Seattle with Mary Ann Wells and in New York with Michel Fokine's sister-in-law, Alexandra Fedorova, who had graduated from St. Petersburg's Imperial School of Ballet. He enrolled as a student in Lincoln Kirstein's and George Balanchine's School of American Ballet and also took classes in modern dance from May O'Donnell, former soloist and dancer of principal roles with the Martha Graham Company from 1932 to 1938.

At nineteen he made his professional debut in Paris. Roland Petit hired him to dance in *Les Ballets de Paris,* 1939. *Les Ballets de Paris* were a revolution in French choreography and dance technique. Roland Petit and his fiery young wife and partner, Zizi Jeanmaire (Renée Jeanmaire), successfully defied the sacrosanct "dance d'ècole" of the Paris Opera Ballet. Roland Petit Ballets became world famous for a dramatic dance pantomime of *Carmen* with Jeanmaire blazing in the title role.

This was valuable training for the nineteen-year-old American dancer from Seattle. In 1950 he joined the faculty of the New York High School for the Performing Arts, an academy to which

* The Robert Joffrey Ballet was renamed City Center Joffrey Ballet in 1966.

117

students were admitted by examination only. He taught ballet and he choreographed dances that were class exercises for his students. Among his most distinguished pupils were Edward Villella and Jonathan Watts.

In the mid-fifties Trudy Goth, one-time pupil of Harald Kreutzberg, dancer with the Ballet Jooss, dance director, writer and a few friends put together the Choreographers Workshop, a showcase for the many hopeful young creators of dance works inspired by the success of ballet in opera houses and musical comedies. Auditions were held in a loft on 6th Avenue and 12th Street in New York on Sunday mornings at eleven. It was hoped that Lincoln Kirstein and Lucia Chase would come. They didn't, but William Kolodney, director of the 92nd Street Y, did.

The auditorium of the 92nd Street Y on Lexington Avenue had excellent acoustics. Its shallow, long stage was just the place for T. S. Eliot reading "The Love Song of J. Alfred Prufrock" and "The Waste Land" and for Dylan Thomas's radio play "Under Milk Wood." The severe, chaste hall, however, was plainly not suited to theatre in any form. But beggars like the Choreographers Workshop were grateful for William Kolodney's generous permission to let them present a bill of dance at the Y twice a year (1954–55). There was no curtain at the Y. No scenery. And no lighting. The faithful came to the performances, few others.

But the word got around that Robert Joffrey's spoof of *Pas de Quatre* by Jules Perrot and Cesare Pugni, the old Valentine ballet that Queen Victoria had commanded in 1845, was fun and charming. Lucia Chase saw it, liked it, and had it performed by Ballet Theatre in 1956.

Joffrey added a male dancer and a thread of story to his version of the contest of ballerinas. In the original *Pas de Quatre* the four ballerinas dance for the queen but no prize is awarded. In *Pas des Déesses* a male dancer as Paris refuses to choose between the goddesses. Is no other Troy at hand? Women's Lib please note.

In the fall of '56 the group renamed Robert Joffrey's Theatre Dancers went on tour in the United States. The Joffrey dancers toured the country every season from '56 to '64 dancing works by George Balanchine (*Pas de Dix*) and Antony Tudor (*Soirée Musicale*) as well as the dances of its own choreographers, Joffrey, Gerald Arpino (the company's leading male dancer), and others. *Pas des Déesses* was later performed by the Ballet Rambert in

London, 1955, by the Ballet Theatre in 1956, and remains in the repertoire of the Robert Joffrey Ballet.

In 1962, cosponsored by the Rebekah Harkness Foundation and the State Department, the Robert Joffrey Ballet was sent on a tour of the Near East, India, and Pakistan. In 1963, the Soviet government invited the Joffrey Ballet to tour the U.S.S.R. On this tour the company danced contemporary works only, notably Alvin Ailey's *Feast of Ashes,* a dramatic pantomime, based on Garcia Lorca's *The House of Bernada Alba* and Gerald Arpino's *Partita for Four,* and *Ropes* with a score by Charles Ives.

In 1965, the Robert Joffrey Ballet was reformed with new sponsorship by Alexander Ewing and the Ford Foundation. Arpino became assistant director and principal choreographer. As official resident company of the New York City Center, the one-time Mecca Temple on West 55th Street, "the Joffrey" spent part of each year in Seattle-Tacoma and performed in the Northwestern states.

It found and has kept a young, eager audience from every cultural tradition and from every walk of life, an audience that rejects "the stale and the stuffy," a phrase that nicks the image of the refined and elite American Ballet Theatre and New York City Ballet.

The ballets by Robert Joffrey (with one exception, *Astarte,* 1967) were not the strongest in the company's repertory. Among those which preceded *Astarte* were *Pas des Déesses, Persephone, Umpateedle* (created for the 1953 Jacob's Pillow Festival), *Le Bal Masqué* (Poulenc score), *Harpsichord Concerto* (de Falla), *Pierrot Lunaire* (Schöenberg), *Le Bal* (Chabrier), *Kaleidoscope* (George Gershwin), *Gamelan* (Lou Harrison). Full of joie de vivre and goodwill they are for the most part carefully wrought, semiromantic, semiclassic vignettes better suited to opera than to musical comedy or music hall. Joffrey was appointed choreographer for the New York City Opera Company (1957–62) and he staged the dances (in which his company appeared) for the Dallas City Opera production of Handel's *Alcina,* in which Joan Sutherland made her American debut (1960).

An admirable company director and teacher, Robert Joffrey was a modest enough man to encourage stronger talents than his own in dance and choreography, notably Gerald Arpino, Anna Sokolow, Christian Holder, Alvin Ailey, Eliot Feld, Twyla Tharp; and he was imaginative enough to compose the psychedelic pas de deux *Astarte* with strip tease and movie shot background, a rock and mixed media blockbuster in the colloquial idiom that reflected, vigorously, the social changes of the time.

Astarte, like Persephone, the heroine of Robert Joffrey's first dance work is a supernatural being. As moon goddess her territory is night and its mysteries, and her arrival at West 55 Street, New York City on September 20, 1967, stirred things up. How to provide the proper amenities? Without any fussing Robert Joffrey used what was at hand. A West Coast rock band to serenade the lady. For her boudoir or alcove mirror—a moving picture that would reflect and enlarge the goings on. For chandeliers—multicolored floodlights. Very pretty and very Mod.

Be it in the 4th century B.C. or in the age of the astronaut, he who falls under the spell of a moon goddess is in a trance. Why bother with fancy words like *psychedelic?* It's a plain fact that at such a time a man's soul is not his own. It belongs to the waiting She.

The young male in Joffrey's *Astarte* strode to the stage from an orchestra seat. He had on an everyday suit that he took off with pride and great deliberation. The love making pas de deux —courtship, retreat, pause, seizure, ecstasy—was handsomely executed by Trinette Singleton in tattooed tights and Maximiliano Zomoso in a loin cloth. Their every move and facial expression was magnified and multiplied in the moving picture mirror behind them. Frozen in the formaldehyde of rock, their bodies are midgets on display before the giant gadget.

The moral of this dramatic skit or fable in contemporary local dialect is a pretty old one, of course. The young man walks away and wakes up out of his trance—in the street, a place of human dimension.

The dance critics called *Astarte* a theatre piece. The drama critics don't review music hall theatre. *Variety* may, one of these days. It was founded to do that in the early 1900s.

GERALD ARPINO

The Joffrey Ballet's assistant director and chief choreographer was born in Staten Island of Italian parents in 1928. The youngest of a family of eight, all music lovers, he was taken to the Metropolitan Opera by an uncle who was an opera singer. Gerald sang in the church choir, and sang in school plays and musicals. Dancing? No. His Catholic family ruled stage dancing out as sinful. He came to dance by accident, after he joined the Coast Guard at seventeen and was sent to Seattle, where he served during World War II. Because Bob Joffrey's mother and his mother were friends, Arpino looked Joffrey up—and came to see him take class at the Mary Ann Wells School. Before long Gerald Arpino was jumping ship. One day, Mary Ann Wells needed a reader for speaking parts in a children's play. The cast did not dance and speak at the same time. Would Gerald read? Yes. Gerald Arpino's premiere in a dance work was a spoken part, the interpretation of a text, the voice of goblins, witches, and children. (A preparation for the dance cantatas to come, and for the spoken poetry in later dance works.) He took dance lessons with Mary Ann Wells after that premiere, the first lesson in his Coast Guard uniform, with other adult beginners, at night.

The war over, Arpino went back to New York. He enrolled in the School of the American Dance, studied with May O'Donnell, Gertrude Shurr, Martha Graham, and Antony Tudor, and danced in everybody's work for free. When Robert Joffrey assembled his ballet company in the early fifties Gerald Arpino was tapped—to be a principal dancer.

In an interview that probed what he was after as a dancer and choreographer Arpino said he wanted to be a combination of Hugh Laing, Igor Youskevitch, Erik Bruhn—"plus himself," and that he wanted his choreography "to provide a way for the American male dancer." In his opinion the male must lead in American dance, a happy state of affairs unrealized by Balanchine and Tudor, who had choreographed so much and so particularly for the American female dancer. Arpino was describing a dilemma that has puzzled many distinguished observers of American dance and American dancers.

Why, for all its steadiness and exactitudes of rhythm, its reticence of phrasing, its clarity and sweep, did American dance style lack imaginative characterization, breadth, and universality?

Is this criticism another way of saying that American dancing has stubbornly resisted "ballet style?" That it is basically folk, acrobatic, and character dancing and that the American male dancer does not see himself or feel at ease in the role of a prince, a mythological god, or an epic hero?

Trained in classic ballet by Balanchine, in pantomime drama by Antony Tudor, in modern dance technique by Martha Graham and her colleagues, Arpino's choreography (he created twenty-eight dance works from 1961 to 1975) has seesawed between neo-Petipa, dramatic pantomime, acrobatics, and a return to dump-and-slab variety acts in the contemporary rock, jazz, and porno idiom. A facile creator of instant theatre, Arpino does not develop the characters he invents. In work that is often allegorical he treats his characters as personified abstractions. The gesture of an Arpino character is not the expression of an emotion that a character has felt or is feeling. A review of some of Arpino's major ballets may reveal other strengths.

In the 1966 fall season at the New York City Center, there were five Arpino ballets in the Joffrey repertoire: *Olympics, Viva Vivaldi!, Incubus, Sea Shadow, Nightwings.* The first two had no story line. The last three were danced and mimed vignettes.

Olympics, with a commissioned score by Toshiro Mayuzumi, is a danced ode to athletics that never quite makes it out of the gym. An all male ballet, it has hints of imaginative characterization, but the hints never become revelations of who, what, where, when, or why. There are glimpses of a Roman chariot driver, of an aerialist, of a tumbler, and of a world of canvas, flapping ropes, and muddy sawdust. For a split second that circus smell is back. But a sketchy outline isn't enough to hold the work together. The young American male dancers canter off like a team breaking out of its dugout into the stadium arena. *Olympics* is fun. It's boys rehearsing for a pageant in half time at a football game. Arpino has not created the young American warrior, nor the young American athlete in *Olympics.* He has created a first-rate finale for a music hall or variety bill.

The choreography for *Viva Vivaldi!* was a solid, workmanlike job of fitting patterns of dancing to the music of the Baroque period's supreme lyricist. Antonio Vivaldi blended two conflicting styles: the old polyphonic with no one voice predominating and the newer monodic style in which a top voice monopolizes attention and reduces all other voices to accompaniment. The eighteenth-century composer and the twentieth-century choreographer-dancer got along very well indeed in *Viva Vivaldi!* The ballet is a fine genre piece. The 1966 critics (British and American) reproached Arpino for "lacking an individual signature in his abstract dance works." They said he was no Balanchine. Be that as it may, *Viva Vivaldi!* remains in the repertoire as a delightful curtain raiser.

The vignettes, *Incubus, Sea Shadow, Nightwings,* show the influence of Roland Petit and French symbolism and surrealism. *Incubus* explores a young girl's mind. Is she possessed by evil or is she having a nightmare—and if so what truth does the nightmare tell?

In *Sea Shadow,* a young man encounters a nymph (or is he dreaming?) on the seashore. The likeness to Mallarmé needs no emphasis. *Nightwings* was set to music by John La Montaine. Balanchine's comment on this work was: "The timeless other world of nature is both the subject and the poetical idea of the piece." La Montaine's score is an attempt to re-create bird song, forest murmur, the chuckle of a running brook, the sigh or rustle of air. Arpino's scenario is about a young man who lives on the top floor of a Soho walk-up with a view of water towers and electric sign boards. The young man's soul is as bleak as the room but for a birdcage, symbol of the timeless other world of nature. While he tosses on his shabby bed a bird woman and her attendants enter. He dances with her. Will she stay? As in the beloved old myth will a wish be granted, will a savior arrive? He has her in his arms. Then, suddenly, her attendants tear her from him. (As in Roland Petit's cat ballet, *Les Demoiselles de la Nuit,* which surely influenced Arpino, there is no integration between nature and the society of man.) Arpino's scenario ends with the murder of the young man by the bird woman.

Whether nightmare or a fable *Nightwings* is full of theatrical invention. But as in *Olympics* the characters have no dimension. Will this weakness cripple Arpino or will he find himself in the lyric theatre?

In *Clowns,* 1968, score by Hershy Kay, the principal character, Everyman, is a clown. As the ballet opens, he witnesses the end of the world by fire (a recorded explosion). Limp clown bodies drop from the sky. Everyman, the chief clown, makes a neat pile of the victims, witnesses their rebirth, their new cycle of life, and once more their death in a plastic gas chamber. The curtain goes down on his solitary figure.

As every dance critic said and perhaps had to say in defense of the profession *Clowns* was all theatre and no dance. "Arpino's choreography is paper thin." Granted. Arpino is no Jerome Robbins. His characters have the bloodless quality of allegory and parable. But Arpino's allegories and parables are about the fears, hopes, and longings of our time in a folk idiom. They would work very well as Street Theatre.

One is reminded of eighteenth-century France when actors and dancers took to the street to survive the monopoly of a state theatre. It's union monopoly and the academic dance monopoly now—*"Le plus ça change le plus c'est la même chose."*

Trinity, 1968, Arpino says, is not a ballet about the youth movement of the sixties, it is a "happening" out of it. Berkeley was the starting point and then we had Kent State; that was the catalyst. The peace marches, the songs that were sung on the streets, all went into *Trinity*.

In the *Relativity of Icarus*, 1974, Arpino reworks the classic myth about Icarus, the reckless youth who defied Daedalus, his father, flew too near the Sun and crashed to his death. In Arpino's version Icarus kills Daedalus.

The ballet is in four parts. A solo for the Sun danced by a Joffrey company ballerina, a long gymnastic pas de deux for Icarus and Daedalus, with song accompaniment, the Sun again in solo, and a finale pas de deux in which Icarus kills his father. The Sun shines in full splendor.

"The audience was thrilled," wrote Arlene Croce, dance critic for *The New Yorker*. "Arpino has gone pretty far this time, and probably will go farther still." She writes further. "He has done rock orgies and peace vigils, doomsday machines, holocausts, and Jesus-freak weddings—all of which remain in repertory to maintain the company's reputation as popular, accessible, and hip. He ought to do a full-evening opus called *Zeitgeist*."

Language as racy as this from the pages of our arbiter of literary etiquette is no mean compliment. It seems to acknowledge that the Joffrey Ballet's programs of ethnic, folk, jazz, and genre dance have renewed an anemic dance vocabulary. Once more, theatre dance confounds the academy.

ALVIN AILEY

Born in Rogers, Texas, 1931

Before he choreographed *Feast of Ashes* for the Robert Joffrey Ballet in 1962, Alvin Ailey had danced in California and at Jacob's Pillow with the Lester Horton Company. He had appeared as featured dancer in Broadway musicals (*The House of Flowers, Jamaica,* and in Harry Belafonte's *Sing, Man, Sing*). He had given concerts of his own work at the 92nd Street YMHA with 35 "incredible" dancers. John Martin, *New York Times* dance critic, gave *Blues Suite, Revelations, Latin Dances,* and a solo dedicated to Lester Horton danced by Ailey himself such good notices that Ailey decided to found his own company, the American Dance Theatre. That was in 1960.

The American Dance Theatre dazzled Europe, Asia, and Australia. It was a smash hit in Paris and in London, its home audience grew and grew and grew. In the summer of '75 it played the State Theatre at Lincoln Center, taking over from the New York City Ballet and the American Ballet Theatre; after the State Theatre season it went on to Paris to play at the Palais du Sport and returned to give a program of blues, jazz, spirituals, and "the black experience" at the East Hampton High School (Long Island) for the benefit of the prestigious East Hampton Guild Hall.

When asked what inspired him to create this great theatre Alvin Ailey says "blood memories." Blood memories were and are the remembrance of a childhood in a small Texas town in the Depression years of the thirties when a black child and his mother lived around with relatives because his father was not there.

He went to a black school across the railroad track, to the Saturday night place (the Dew-Drop-Inn), "with everybody else" for the country dancing and singing. On Sunday he went to the Baptist Church where the congregation shouted in praise of God.

What turned the small boy on was the church ritual, and the Saturday night performances of dancing and ballad singing by itinerant folk singers.

Here was the oldest form of theatre, acts of praise, propitiation, and sacrifice, and out of it came the American Dance Theatre of Alvin Ailey.

After this came Ailey's training as a dancer, a choreographer, and a theatre man.

His mother moved to Los Angeles in the forties. There was work there in airplane factories. At the Los Angeles school, Alvin played football, wrote poetry, and became proficient in gymnastics. He also went to the movies, and the sight of Gene Kelly and Fred Astaire dancing the musicals of the forties on Hollywood's Silver Screen made a dancer of him, much as Anna Pavlowa dancing in schools and music halls, twenty-six years earlier, had made little American girls dream of toe shoes and tutus.

A friend took Alvin to the Lester Horton School in Hollywood. After a good deal of seesawing between a career in the teaching of Romance languages (a strong second interest) and a career in dance and theatre Alvin accepted a scholarship and went to work for Lester Horton.

Lester Horton, born in Indianapolis, had studied dance there and also in Chicago with Adolph Bolm, a graduate of the St. Petersburg Imperial School of the Ballet. Horton began his professional career as a theatrical designer and stage manager for the Indianapolis Civic Theatre. From early youth to his death at the age of forty-seven, he was fascinated by the American Indian. He became an authority on the subject. He studied Iroquois, Red River, Penobscot, Ojibwa tribal dances and ceremonials first hand. He was asked to design and play the leading role in a pageant based on Longfellow's *Hiawatha,* produced in California. The *San Francisco Examiner* critic, Redfern Mason, wrote: "The music is tribal, the dances and ceremonies are authentic. . . . it was like slipping away from this workaday world into that folk life which is the primitive poetry of America."

The poetry of folk life. A gift for understanding that poetry united the restless young black man and the equally restless and gifted creator of the Lester Horton Dance Theatre. Horton had worked with Michio Ito and used techniques of Japanese as well as Indian dance. He acted in William Butler Yeats's *Hawk's Well,* inspired by a Japanese noh play.

Horton's bold experiments with modern dance techniques interested new audiences. His students were a league of cultures and nations, Mexican, Japanese, Spanish, black, and white. The dances that Lester Horton choreographed were inspired by Mexican themes, by Paul Klee, by Garcia Lorca, by the music of Stravinsky and Duke Ellington. Alvin Ailey watched, listened, learned. He taught the children's classes at the Lester Horton School. When Horton died of a heart attack in 1953, Ailey and the business manager tried to keep the school and the company going. After one year they had to give up. Ted Shawn and Walter Terry called Alvin Ailey's first long, formless works (presented at Jacob's Pillow) "kitchen sink" ballets. Then a telephone call came from Philadelphia. George Balanchine had just been let go as choreographer of the musical adaptation of Truman Capote's

House of Flowers. Herbert Ross, his replacement, wanted Alvin Ailey and Carmen de Lavallade, the stars of the Horton company, to be the lead dancers in *House of Flowers.* One training period was over.

And now a review of Alvin Ailey's accomplishment, which in this writer's opinion is very great and twofold.

The greatness being *first* the immense range in theme, subject matter, and form of his so-called ballets, which are in effect no-nonsense music hall acts, and *second* his ability as an impressario. Ailey has done for modern dance choreographers and dancers what Serge Diaghilev did for the choreographers and dancers of the Fokine revolution; he has created a repertory company and commanded a world audience.

It is often said by the very best critics that Ailey's most notable works are "the beautiful and moving suite of dances to spirituals."* What is referred to, of course, is the folk poetry of his blood memories. It is true that blood memories are always the most moving, whether in folk art or in classic literature. What comes to mind is Marcel Proust's famed novel about time remembered, *Swann's Way,* with its memories of Combray (Illiers), of the tall church spire that commanded cobbled streets, the little town, the chateau, the river, the east wind rippling the wheat fields, and that evoked twelve centuries of French history. *Swann's Way* is the most poetical section of *A la recherche du temps perdu.* But it's not the whole story. Anymore than *Blues Suite* and *Revelations* are all Alvin Ailey has to say.

Ariette Oubliée, the title of a poem by Paul Verlaine, is also the title of a dance work by Alvin Ailey. *Ariette* (a little song) was on the bill at Ailey's first full scale concert at the 92nd Street Y, New York City in December '58, along with *Blues Suite, Cinco Latinos,* and *Revelations.* Set to the music of Claude Debussy *Ariette Oubliée* is a variation on one of Ailey's major themes: simplicity and feeling.

Like the French impressionist and symbolist poet, Ailey is an antirhetoric man. Verlaine's limpid songs wrang the neck of the too bombastic nineteenth-century French verse just as Ailey's profoundly human dance theatre brushes aside the overelaborate technique and high-power gymnastics of some twentieth-century ballet and modern dance choreographers.

---

* John Percival, *Modern Ballet* (Dutton, 1970).

Paul Verlaine's *Ariette Number III's* first lines:

> It's weeping in my heart
> Like it's raining over the town
> *(Il pleure dans mon coeur*
> *Comme il pleut sur la ville)*

is to an ode by Victor Hugo what an Ailey dance work is to a Balanchine-Stravinsky ballet or to a Martha Graham ritual dance. The French lyric poet and the American dancer and choreographer express very basic feelings in simple, contemporary language.

In *Feast of Ashes,* '62, *Ariadne,* '65, and *The River,* '70, Ailey uses new subject matter and more elaborate forms.

Feast of Ashes is Garcia Lorca's *The House of Bernada Alba* in dance and pantomime set to the music of the Mexican composer Carlos Surinach. Lorca's tragic telling of the sacrifice of two lovers to the authority of a matriarch who is the symbol of the family honor loses its grandeur in Alvin Ailey's and Carlos Surinach's version. More like an Orozco mural than a Goya, *Feast of Ashes* has many of the same qualities as a Palace vaudeville dramatic sketch of the twenties. It introduces scenes from the work of a major writer to a popular audience. Robert Mantell and Genevieve Hamper did the same in their great scenes from *MacBeth,* and so did Ethel Barrymore, who toured the vaudeville circuit in Sir James Barrie's *Twelve Pound Look,* a Women's Lib protest if ever there was one.

The River, commissioned by Ballet Theatre and danced by its company, is a suite of dances by Alvin Ailey set to music by Duke Ellington. Ellington is quoted as saying that he and Ailey take the river (it would seem to be the Mississippi) symbolically. But not as T. S. Eliot took that same river, not as a "strong, brown god. . . . sullen, untamed and intractable. . . . unpropiti-ated. . . . waiting."

Ailey and Ellington's river is a life force, not a symbol of an angry slave plotting revenge on an overingenious, domineering master. Ailey and Ellington's river rises, meanders, finds its mainstream, and finally the sea. *The River* seems to say that man and nature share life not as master and slave but as fellow passengers in the cycle of time.

There is not a great distance in miles between T. S. Eliot's birthplace in St. Louis, Missouri, and Alvin Ailey's birthplace in Rogers, Texas. Both were born and were boys in the Southwest of the United States. And although their interpretation of nature varies there is very little difference in the rhythm and vocabulary of Eliot's best work and that of Ailey's best choreography. Eliot's jazz rhythms and colloquialisms turned Victorian poetry upside down. In *The River,* jive and boogie, jitter and can-can move right in with classic adagio.

Like T. S. Eliot, Alvin Ailey "can do the police [read the police gazette] in many voices." Both are masters of the low comedy vernacular. A great accomplishment. Occasionally, though, Ailey's mastery of the vernacular almost runs away with the meaning of a work. An exhibition of method seems to come first, which is no more acceptable in a popular work than in a high-brow entertainment.

When "the Ailey" played the State Theatre at Lincoln Center for the first time in August '74 much was made (somewhat too much, perhaps) of its stated purpose: To explore and reveal the black experience and to keep certain modern dance works, from Denishawn to neo-Martha Graham, alive and well.

But this stated purpose raises some questions. Will as gifted and imaginative a choreographer as Alvin Ailey, and a man of his culture, be willing and able to keep himself and his company boxed up within the limits of ethnic and character dancing (with a few music hall turns thrown in)?

And if the answer is "yes," how will Ailey and his company and also the Joffrey, Merce Cunningham, and Paul Taylor survive the competition of the new Nijinsky, Rudolf Nureyev, whose animal grace and power have given the American male an image of himself as danseur noble, and culture hero much as every young girl in America dreamt of herself as a classic ballerina after seeing Anna Pavlowa dance?

CHAPTER X

AMERICAN MODERN DANCE
1945–75

MARTHA GRAHAM

". . . roughly in the middle 1930's, the American Modern Dance (a lyric art) attained its peak and enjoyed a creative harvest on the high plateau that had been its first goal (a revelation of some aspect of the dancer's relation to a universal truth). [Note: Winthrop Palmer's parentheses.] The dynamic possibilities of American Modern Dance, however, made it impossible to rest there, even though pushing onward could only mean the pursuit of a new goal and a descent from the peak. The road . . . led toward the theatre, with Graham in the van of the march."*

In the 1920s, with the help of her first dancing teachers, Ted Shawn and Ruth St. Denis, Martha Graham made her stage debut in vaudeville. *Xochitl*, a pre-Columbian legend dramatized by Shawn, in which Graham played the title role, was booked by the Pantages Vaudeville Circuit and toured the West Coast. It had a commissioned score by Homer Grunn and sets by the Mexican artist Francisco Cornajo. True to classic definition of vaudeville as low comedy in colloquial, contemporary idiom Shawn choreographed the story of a dancing girl who gets to be Empress (after trial by fires of lust), in the recherché Art Nouveau style that was then "the rage." Graham's solo dance performed with Batik scarf, flutter, melting pose, and arch attitude was more *tableau vivant* than movement. But the audiences loved it, and they loved the heavy pantomime of the pas de deux (Shawn-Graham) and

---

* John Martin, "American Modern Dance," *Dance Encyclopedia*, ed. by Anatole Chujoy and P. W. Manchester (Simon and Schuster, 1967).

the glamor of the pre-Columbian scenery, costumes, and lighting. It was romantic, lush vaudeville. The writer, at the benefit performance of Graham's ballet *Lucifer,* with Nureyev in the title role and Margot Fonteyn as his partner, in a series of superb tableaux under billowing scarves by Halston, was instantly back at a Denishawn production.

Much has been written about Martha Graham's vocabulary of movement and the technique required for its use, a vocabulary and a technique she created in the late twenties and early thirties after quitting John Murray Anderson's Greenwich Village Follies, Broadway, and the Denishawn oriental lyricism of her Follies numbers. What has seldom been written is that Graham's vocabulary of movement was a modification of the dance style of Mary Wigman, the great German expressionist dancer. Mary Wigman, built on the lines of a Gothic cathedral saint, had a Gothic saint's austere grace. Her dance movement was hieratic and tragic, an expression of noble resignation to an unhappy fate.

Graham, a pugnacious Celt, used the expressionist style to challenge fate. Graham vocabulary and technique were based on contest, the struggle with outer and inner foes.

Graham technique was acquired by the practice of exercises on and off the floor similar to the gymnastic exercises of ancient Greece, a systematic physical discipline designed to develop and exhibit dexterity, strength, and control in the use of the body. The Graham dancer, often a physical education major, was trained to move like an athlete prepared for combat. Muscular rhythm and breathing had priority over music. Music was an afterthought. Commissioned scores served as footnotes, punctuation marks, or stress. They underlined an action or heightened a mood. An honorable assistant like the set, the costumes, and the lighting, American Modern Dance music was not asked to inspire a dance movement or to give the so-called dancer another dimension. What saved Martha Graham's new dance vocabulary from being just a handsome display of gymnastics and of ingenious baroque plastique was the choreographer's incontestable genius for mime.

In 1946 she prepared a script on the subject of Jason and Medea for a festival of contemporary music. Samuel Barber wrote the score. Called *Cave of the Heart* it was a small-scale work for four dancers: Jason (Erick Hawkins), Medea (Graham), the young princess (Yuriko), and the chorus (May O'Donnell), who commented on the actions of the principals.

Don McDonagh wrote about it: "For herself, Graham created

one of the most venomous parts in her repertory. . . . Because Jason prefers the young princess Medea kills him. . . . (not her rival as in the classic story). Graham's solo, in which she extracted a long red ribbon from herself, simulated the spewing up of a vile liquid having the corrosive power of acid. Noguchi prepared . . . a brass harness with quivering brass rays emanating from it which Medea took upon herself after the murder. Moving about in it she was like a glittering, malevolent presence. The piece was the incarnation of jealousy and signaled a turn on Graham's part. . . ."* Graham had turned from vaudeville performance to actress of classic tragedy.

After *Cave of the Heart* the repertory of the Graham Company became in large measure a contradiction. In new work after new work America's Sarah Bernhardt played classic tragedy with a supporting cast of gymnasts, acrobats, folk dancers, and mimes. There was fall from high place in a setting of circus and vaudeville. Graham's partners in *Errand into the Maze* (the Minotaur legend), *Night Journey* (the Oedipus story), *Clytemnestra, Alcestis*, and *Phaedra* and other works were Erick Hawkins and Merce Cunningham. Erick was built more like Abraham Lincoln than like Jason or other members of the Greek mythological aristocracy, and Merce, part clown, part faun, was a creature out of *A Midsummer Night's Dream.*

How could such a mixture of styles, methods, and meaning work? For a while there was resistance—hooting, scoffing, boredom, in the west, the middle west, and in Paris and London. Then little by little the resistance stopped. Graham's new vocabulary found its public, on tour in the Near East, in the Far East, and in a second season in London, in 1963.

The first season in London, 1954, was a major flop. Only one critic, Richard Buckle, made any sense out of the "abstractions and philosophies of Miss Graham's dance dramas." Buckle, writing for the weekly Sunday newspaper *The Observer,* urged all habit-encrusted people in need of "a third eye" to watch Martha Graham, for "she has enlarged the language of the soul." Buckle was not "exhausted" as his colleagues were by the new language that said new things.

There was really nothing very new about Graham's basic theme, the conflict of passion and duty, of man's desires and his ideals. But she did express that conflict in the new and violent

* Don McDonagh, *Martha Graham, A Biography* (New York: Praeger, 1973).

language of gymnastic allegory that suited a time inching back to the Middle Ages. For all her use of Greek myth Graham was creating the folk theatre of a miracle and morality play.

Of course London was better acquainted with the miracle play as a theatre form than were New York, Washington, San Francisco, and Hollywood, and her second time around in Britain things were different for Martha Graham.

"Taste had changed," wrote John Percival, ballet critic of the *London Times* in a comment about Graham's second visit to London. "She enjoyed a wild success," he went on, "not only with the general public but with dancers, artists and theatre people on whom her innovations exerted an influence such as she had never known before."

Graham had bowled over one Englishman at the time of her first London season. Robin Howard, a hotel and restaurant proprietor, made the second season possible. He put up his own money, he persuaded Lord Harewood, director of the Edinburgh Festival, to raise five thousand pounds, he hired a theater on short notice, the Prince of Wales, and after the season's triumphant close he asked Graham to audition dancers who would study with her in the United States, return to England, found a Graham style of school, and eventually a company.

Graham agreed. Howard paid travel and living expenses. Graham gave free lessons.

In 1969, six years after Robin Howard made Graham's second season possible, the London Contemporary Dance Ensemble performed in its own theater, the Palace. The head of the British Arts Council, Lord Goodman presided at the official opening. The major dance work presented was *El Penitente*.

Graham chose *Legend of Judith* for her company's premiere at the Prince of Wales Theatre. She did not dance the role of the proud murderess who decapitated her people's conqueror, the five-star Babylonian general Holofernes, he whom she had lured into her tent and bed. At sixty-nine Graham was not doing much dancing. She acted. And as the head of Holofernes rolled out of a scarlet blanket wrapped about the avenging queen and a headless corpse lurked in the background, the audiences at the Prince of Wales and elsewhere were shaken with pity and terror.

Understandably America's first tragedienne was reluctant (who would have felt otherwise in her place) to let younger members of the company take over her roles in the scenes from great classic literature she had dramatized herself. The company was, after all, her company, not a full-scale variety theatre like the Palace with an impressario like Albee who booked acts. The Graham Company was, perhaps, a troupe, a troupe of gifted dancers, acrobats and the greatest of mimes who might just be announcing a theatre to come.

CHAPTER XI

DEFECTORS FROM THE GRAHAM COMPANY

MAY O'DONNELL, GERTRUDE SHURR,
ANNA SOKOLOW

The first ones to go were women, members of the group who had danced "Amazon" dances with Graham for ten years.

May O'Donnell, Gertrude Shurr, and Anna Sokolow left to found their own companies when Graham dropped lyric American modern dance for dramatically inspired theatre dance, modified her percussion line, "took on" Erick Hawkins, and introduced sex in dances between Hawkins and herself. A defector from ballet and Balanchine, Erick Hawkins was fifteen years younger than Martha.

O'Donnell, Shurr, and Sokolow remained true to Modern Dance as dancers, choreographers, and teachers, to dance as movement not dependent on music or other forms. They did not, however, perpetuate the "Amazon" dances kin to the ecstatic or religious dance of primitive societies. Each in her own way made some accommodation with theatre and found herself in the sixties teaching Modern Dance technique to Robert Joffrey, Gerald Arpino, Alvin Ailey, and others, or having her work performed by ballet companies.

The May O'Donnell Dance Company appeared in New York and on tour in the United States. O'Donnell and Shurr put together the San Francisco Dance Theatre in '39. O'Donnell toured with the José Limón Company, and was guest artist of the Graham Company in '44–'52. She created the great secondary roles of Pioneer Woman in *Appalachian Spring*, She of the Earth

135

in *Dark Meadow,* the Attendant in *Herodiade,* and Chorus in *Cave of the Heart.* O'Donnell also danced principal roles in Graham's famous dance pantomimes, *Letter to the World, Deaths and Entrances, Punch and the Judy, Every Soul is a Circus,* and *Primitive Mysteries.* She also joined the faculty of the prestigious New York High School of the Performing Arts, whose graduates joined ballet companies, modern dance companies, or Broadway theatre.

Anna Sokolow, while a member of the Graham Company, found time to teach at the Neighborhood Playhouse as assistant to Louis Horst and to give performances of her own choreography with her own dance group.

In '39 Sokolow accepted an invitation from the Ministry of Fine Arts of Mexico to give performances in Mexico City. It was to be a six-week season. At the end of a year Anna Sokolow was still in Mexico. She put together Mexico's first modern dance group and spent six months of the year in Mexico for the next nine years ('39–'49) training dancers and creating solos and group works. Among the notable solos were: *Mexican Retablo, Lament for the Death of a Bullfighter, Kadisch.* The group works were created for the Ballet de Bellas Artes, a cultural institution supported by the poets, painters, and composers of Mexico.

The vivid repertoire of Ballet de Bellas Artes was principally inspired by Mexican and Indian folklore. Sokolow choreographed contemporary works: *El Renacujo Paseador* with music by Silvestre Revueltas and *Antigona* with music by Carlos Chavez. In '61 she staged *Opus 60* (music by the jazz composer Teo Macero) for Bellas Artes, also *Dreams* (Webern) and *Musical Offering* (Bach).

In 1954, Sokolow reassembled a company of actor-dancers in the United States. She was no longer dancing but the company performed her works at intervals: *Rooms* (Kenyon Hopkins) '55; *Metamorphosis* (a dramatization of Franz Kafka's story) '57; *Opus* (Teo Macero) '58; and *Dreams* (Webern) '61, a dance that in Sokolow's words was "an indictment of Nazi Germany."

Many ballet and dance companies presented and present works by Anna Sokolow: the Nederlands Dance Theater, the Joffrey Ballet, the Alvin Ailey Dance Theater. She has worked in Israel with the Yemenite Company Imbal, has created dances for the Broadway theatre and for the New York City Opera. The Lena Robbins Foundation backed a two-week season of her work at the Off-Broadway York Theatre in New York.

What is Anna Sokolow's principal contribution as theatrical dancer-choreographer in mid-twentieth century America? She has said that in her opinion art should be a comment on contemporary life.

Well, given her themes, her subjects, and her idiom (frenetic and jazzy), it would seem that she danced the history and the agony of the Second World War into twentieth-century American theatre as Tony Pastor sang the history of the Civil War into the nineteenth-century music halls of the nation.

ERICK HAWKINS

In the 1940s and 1950s for all the protest of its practitioners American Modern Dance had become an academy. The Martha Graham Company was its first theatre, and Graham, dancer-choreographer-director, ran her troupe much as actor-playwrights-directors had done before her in Italy, London, and at the Rue de Richelieu.

As the style and content of her dance plays changed, as her way of moving changed—less dancing, more acting—her first dancers (male) came and went.

Erick Hawkins, who came in '38, left in '51. He will perhaps be longest remembered for the roles he created in Graham's Victorian-Americana dance works, that curious blend of country and parlor, of frontier breeziness and middle-class mincing that Graham seized and immortalized in *Appalachian Spring* and *Letter to the World*.

The pre-Main Street American man comes alive in all his romantic and sentimental nobility when Hawkins as Pioneer Husband gravely establishes his authority over a little community (Oh Women's Lib) and places a sheltering arm around Graham, his Pioneer Bride.

Hawkins's nineteenth-century American build, his way of holding his handsome head—a bit detached—was just right for Victorian Americana. It lacked the fire needed to play a tragic hero, Greek or other. What more natural, then, than to leave when *Cave of the Heart, Errand into the Maze, Night Journey,* and *Judith* were added to the repertoire, and set up a company of one's own.

Stating that his purpose as a choreographer was to restore pure poetry to movement, a quality lost in the diagram dancing of ballet and the mime of modern dance, Hawkins's dancing tries to blend Isadora Duncan's "Attic grace" and Shanta Rao's tender sensuality. He rejects the "frustration" and the "melodrama" of modern dance, which he describes as expressions of "personal neurosis" that do not reach the truth of tragedy.

A member of Lincoln Kirstein's American Ballet, in 1937, Hawkins danced in Balanchine's *The Card Party,* music by Stravinsky; in Lew Christensen's *Filling Station,* music by Virgil Thomson; and in *Pocahontas,* choreography by Lew Christensen, music by Elliott Carter, Jr. He also choreographed a ballet *Show Piece* for Kirstein's Ballet Caravan, '38, to music by Robert McBride.

He created abstract dance works for his small group after leaving the Graham Company; scholarly critics called these dance compositions "ballets," without plot, without realistic characters; they were true to Hawkins' purpose—a search for pure poetry in movement. The word *poetry* from the Greek *poeia (making)* has come to mean the making of images; in verse or in prose by writers, in space by sculptors, painters, and dancers, in sound by music men; images that reveal a similarity between opposites, a far more useful measurement than the hypotheses and demonstrations of plane or solid geometry. A far more difficult one, unfortunately, which is why there are so many more engineers complete with computers than Shakespeares and Rembrandts and Beethovens and Nijinskys. An engineer whose blueprint is not the hoped for formula for a miracle machine can go back to the tool shop. A choreographer whose dances lack dimension can design graceful decorative tableaux. Which is pretty much what Hawkins has done. At times his concert programs have a Denishawn quality—more illustration (look) than imagination (see). Lucia Dlugoszewski, the composer-pianist, has collaborated with him closely. In the sixties he toured the United States, and danced in London and in Paris at the Theatre des Nations Festival.

The titles of some of his principal dance numbers could be the titles of poems, by Robert Frost, perhaps: *8 Clear Places, Early Floating, inner feet of a summer fly.*

A Carnegie Hall performance of new work in '75 had very mixed reviews.

MERCE CUNNINGHAM

When Martha Graham invited Merce Cunningham, at that

Rudolf Nureyev in *Le Corsair. Louis Peres.*

Rudolf Nureyev in *Lucifer. Martha Swope.*

Firebird with Maria Tallchief and Francisco Moncion. *Walter Owen. Dance Collection, New York Public Library at Lincoln Center, Astor, Lenox and Tilden Foundations.*

Giselle with Tamara Toumanova and Serge Lifar. Ballet Russe de Monte Carlo, 1939. *Dance Collection, New York Public Library at Lincoln Center, Astor, Lenox and Tilden Foundations.*

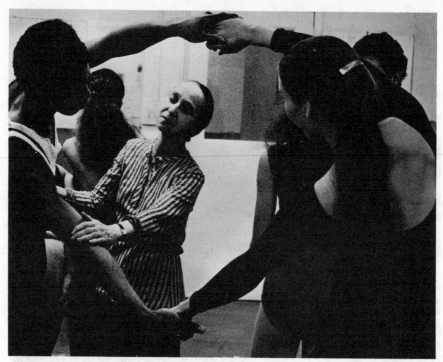

Anna Sokolow with dancers from Contemporary Dance System. *M. B. Hunnewell.*

Robert Joffrey. *Herbert Migdoll.*

Gerald Arpino. *Jack Mitchell.*

Gerald Arpino as a dancer. *Walter Owen. Dance Collection, New York Public Library at Lincoln Center, Astor, Lenox and Tilden Foundations.*

Joffrey Ballet's *Trinity. Herbert Migdoll.*

Merce Cunningham in *Lavish Escapade. Dance Collection, New York Public Library at Lincoln Center, Astor, Lenox and Tilden Foundations.*

Alvin Ailey as a dancer. *Zachary Freyman.*

Alvin Ailey Company in *The River* with Keith Lee. *Martha Swope*.

Paul Taylor in *The Last Flycatcher*. *Zachary Freyman*.

Eliot Feld. *Thomas Victor*.

Eliot Feld in *The Real McCoy. Herbert Migdoll*.

Erick Hawkins in *Minotaur. John Geraci. Dance Collection, New York Public Library at Lincoln Center, Astor, Lenox and Tilden Foundations.*

time his first name was Mercier, to join her company he was very proficient in tap dancing and had a great jump. As vaudeville and nightclub performer he had toured his home state, Washington, also Oregon and California. In 1938, he danced in Lester Horton's *Conquest* at Mills College in San Francisco.

It is said that Cunningham drew immediate attention to himself in all his classes in the dancing school at Mills College run by Louis Horst's wife, Betty. This was where he and Martha Graham met, and where their association as dancers and choreographers began.

Cunningham attended the Graham Summer School in Bennington, Vermont, in '38. The following year Graham began working on a company work in which Merce Cunningham as second male dancer would be pitted against Erick Hawkins. The title of the work was *Every Soul Is a Circus,* a line of poetry by Vachel Lindsay.

In *Circus,* a droll and witty animated cartoon, Graham cast herself as kittenish woman teasing and flirting with her two men, Cunningham the acrobat, Hawkins the ringmaster, while her alter-ego in a modish outfit (Jean Erdman) looked on at the circus goings-on from a box. After much absurd tripping about, confrontation and retreat, kittenish woman chooses the agent of order. He with the whip masters kittenish woman. The airborne acrobat loses. But Merce Cunningham in his first role with the Graham Company had moved into the foreground of modern dance. His speed and his nimble leaping were noticed in the succession of roles given him in the "American" dance works that Graham said had won back audiences "alienated through grimness of theme and a non-theatrical approach to our own dancing."

Did *American Document, Every Soul Is a Circus, Letter to the World, Punch and the Judy, El Penitente* (redesigned by Isamu Noguchi), and *Appalachian Spring* with Martha at fifty playing the young bride, win back an audience frightened away by the murky writhings and contortions of "the long woolens period" of American Modern Dance? Or did this repertoire reassure, with its occasional quotations from classic American prose and poetry, a middle-class America troubled at the challenges of its values by World War II?

Cunningham, in any case, had something else to say. Not interested in middle-class America, or in social realism of any kind, he left the Graham Company in 1945.

In the spring of '44, Merce Cunningham choreographed and danced *Mysterious Adventure,* a solo dance, as part of the Graham Company's program at the National Theatre in New York. Aware of restlessness in the company Graham had sponsored the work of "promising" young dancers. She hoped to head off more defections.

That same spring of '44, two blocks east of the National Theatre, the Ballet Theatre sponsored a new work by a promising young choreographer few years older than Merce Cunningham. The work was *Fancy Free,* the choreographer Jerome Robbins.

It would be twenty years before dance critics and a public made any sense out of Merce's dance idiom. By that time Jerome Robbins had teamed up with the New York City Ballet as assistant artistic director and was working with Leonard Bernstein on a musical called *West Side Story. West Side Story* was Romeo and Juliet as Street Theatre. It was a blockbuster. Robbins's genius for creating character adapted itself to any theatrical form— and *West Side Story*—later a movie—was cheered by critics of music, theatre, dance, and film in the United States and overseas.

Criticism of *Mysterious Adventure* by John Martin of the *New York Times* called the work a "cutish solo and exhibition piece, quite without content, that belonged to the dance recital category." Martin added that it was perhaps more kind than wise for Miss Graham to sponsor young choreographers.

In '44 American Modern Dance was dramatic pantomime by Martha Graham. Acting, pantomime, costume, and stage design had priority over dancing and music. Merce Cunningham had something entirely different in mind. Rejecting realistic mime, symbolic hand props, a narrative line, literary texts, and genre tableaux he set off alone to pioneer with "free" movement in space and time. But not without a thorough training in the basic disciplines of dance. While a soloist with the Graham Company he studied ballet at Lincoln Kirstein's School of the American Ballet in New York and taught a weekly class in Modern Dance at this school in 1947 and 1948. In 1948 Lincoln Kirstein asked him to compose a work for Ballet Society of New York City to music by John Cage, Cunningham's closest friend and collaborator. It was called *The Seasons.* Kirstein called it tender and pretty but without "virtuosic interest." It was not in a new idiom of movement.

Cunningham assembled a small company, among them Paul

Taylor, at Black Mountain College, North Carolina, in '53 and planned a season at the Theatre de Lys in New York City ('53–'54). The Theatre de Lys season, financed with great difficulty, was a flop—not a dance critic came to the week of performances. Cage and Cunningham wrote desperate SOS letters "to friend and foe." The company of six dancers, two musicians, and a stage manager/lighting designer (Robert Rauschenberg) went off to perform whatever dates materialized in a Volkswagen bus.

The next few years were hard and meager but Merce kept right on choreographing and teaching. A Guggenheim fellowship helped. An invitation to perform at the New London, Connecticut, Dance Festival in the summer of '58 was very welcome.

The Festival was a respite from busing. It provided a residence for the company (Carolyn Brown, Remy Charlip, Joanne Melsher, Viola Farber, Marianne Preger, Paul Taylor, Anita Dencks), a guaranteed performance schedule, rehearsal time and space, and an earning power. Cunningham choreographed some of his best work at New London in '58, '59, '60.

The new works were true to Merce's aesthetic, which in his own words was "dance concerned with each single instant as it comes along." The overtones of this philosophy, an analysis of movement like Marcel Duchamp's famous woman coming down stairs, were not acceptable to José Limón, Doris Humphrey, and the directors of the Connecticut Festival. Doris Humphrey and José Limón were dedicated to the principles of humanism, as were most of the dance teachers and students who came to New London. If you had created and were performing *Lament for Ignacio Sanchez Mejias* inspired by Garcia Lorca's poem in honor of the unflinching courage of a bullfighter, or *The Moor's Pavane*, Shakespeare's *Othello* in dance movement, you were impatient and irritated by Cunningham's stopwatch dancing and his casual attitude to music, decor, and lighting.

At the 13th American Dance Festival at New London Cunningham presented *Septet, Night Wandering, Rune, Crises,* and *Suite for Five*. Louis Horst wrote for the *New London Day* that *Septet,* choreographed in '53 and one of Merce Cunningham's most persuasive works, brimming with nonsensical and surprising nonsequiturs, was performed with great esprit by Mr. Cunningham and his brilliant company, Carolyn Brown, Viola Farber, Marilyn Wood, Remy Charlip, and Jack Moore to the consciously nonsensical music of Etik Satie. Mr. Horst thought *Night Wan-*

dering, a duet for Cunningham and Carolyn Brown, was too long and too unvaried in dynamic range. He called its score by Bo Nilsson "agressively dry and arid music." Walter Terry called *Crises,* to music by Conlon Nancarrow, a generally frolicsome bit full of gesture and muscular jokes. What the crises were about was anybody's guess.

At the 14th Connecticut Festival (1961) Merce Cunningham premiered *Aeon.* Louis Horst regretted that the insensitive hulla-balloo of Mr. Cage in the pit "amplified umpteen millions of degrees" made it completely impossible to appreciate Merce Cunningham's solo passages, work that attained the high places of dance "with a fine dramatic expressiveness." "We are apt to make Mr. Cage the Dennis the Menace of this week," the veteran music master of Modern Dance concluded, "but Mr. Cunningham must also share the critical disapproval of many lovers of the arts that cannot be classed as fuddy duddies. Everyone has a right to his own opinions. That is true, but that also includes the critics."

Not surprisingly, the best spots on the Festival program went to the Limón Company as well as the largest share of the Festival budget. Merce and his company quit the Connecticut Festival in the early sixties. There was some bitterness.

Most American ballet and Modern Dance fans know that when Serge Diaghilev brought his Ballet Russes to Paris in May, 1909, the town's art milieu exploded, that the attitudes and gestures of Vaslav Nijinsky's *L'Aprés Midi d'un Faune* established Modern Dance and that a cultural revolution got underway. Fathered by Paul Cézanne, its basic principle declared that nature and solid geometry were one, and that African sculptors had known and put this into practice before anyone had come up with the word *cubism.*

Cubist painter Picasso designed sets for the Diaghilev Ballet, also Georges Rouault, and De Chirico. Fifty years later an emigré French cubist painter, Marcel Duchamp, and his New York en-tourage (William de Kooning, Mark Rothko, Barnett Newman, Richard Lippold, Larry Rivers, James Rosenquist, Andy Warhol, Jasper Johns, and Robert Rauschenberg) advertised a sale of their works to finance a New York season for Merce Cunningham.

The sale brought in forty-five thousand dollars. That was enough for a two-week season on Broadway. But the '62–'63 newspaper strike dimmed Broadway, and Cunningham, Cage, and company went west in the Volkswagen bus. Merce taught and there were performances in California universities. In the fall of '63 John Cage and Merce Cunningham announced they had decided to tour abroad in response to many inquiries. The plans for the New York season were cancelled. The tour abroad, notably the hurrah of the London audience, turned everything around for Merce Cunningham as dancer, if not for the three-ring circus of his so-called independent collaborators—music, decor, lighting.

James Klosty writes that Cunningham's hands-off attitude to his theatrical environment is not a baffling and self-destructive exercise in anarchy nor is it the only modern-day successor to the heritage of Diaghilev's Ballet Russes. "Cunningham is a virtuoso dancer" and the choreographer who added the commonplace movement of daily life to the technique of ballet and the theatrics of Graham. He is the first choreographer "to honor equally the arabesque and the limp."*

Carolyn Brown, for twenty years one of Merce's principal dancers, uses the word *loner* to describe him. He is no collaborator, he works *secretively*; the dancers in his company "discover" the set in the final rehearsal, the music and the lighting in the first performance.**

Was there possibly a gambler in this poet dancer, who dared stake with casual and elegant indifference what *he* created against all comers?

The Cunningham Company tour around the world (there were performances in India, Thailand, and Japan) was privately financed. The United States Cultural Exchange Program had sent José Limón's Company to the Far East the year before and did not respond to appeals from Cunningham and Cage. But as "the gypsy dance troupe" (the Company's words) moved across Europe, the Near East, and Asia performing their eighteen dances there were bright spots—Rauschenberg's prize at the Vienna Biennale, Francis Mason's sponsorship as American Cultural Attaché in London, the Czech government's help, the audiences in Cologne that would not stop shouting.

Dancing in public squares, in museum courtyards, in the

---

* James Klosty, ed., *Merce Cunningham* (Saturday Review Press, E.P. Dutton Inc., 1975).

** "Essays, Stories, and Remarks about Merce Cunningham," *Dance Perspective No. 34* (Summer 1968).

arena of a gym—the young choreographers of the 'seventies learned about that from Merce Cunningham. "Nontheatrical space" was often the only space available on world tours, and Merce arranged his programs accordingly. He assembled whatever parts of his repertoire would fit—choosing "excerpts" from his dance works as classical ballet company directors do.

A private foundation now assures the existence of Cage and Cunningham's company. It has moved to excellent quarters in Westbeth, the artist's housing project in New York City. It tours, it appears locally to much acclaim. In December '75 it shared a season at the Off-Broadway Roundabout Theatre with young companies.

In what category are Merce Cunningham's works? They tell no story. They are not graceful dance suites or ingenious acrobatic structures. They create no immortal characters. To this witness who has seen his early and late work it would seem that as a choreographer Merce has gone from romantic fresco (*Summerspace*) to comic strip satire of the mechanical dismemberment of man in an assembly line society.

PAUL TAYLOR

Born, Pittsburgh, Pa. 1930

Dancing describes images in space. Some are ingenious or graceful decoration, a pleasing visual experience. Some more ambitiously reflect a picture of man out of his everyday rut, be that soldier, sailor, tinker, tailor, etc., and speak to the heart and the conscience.

The so-called abstract dancers provide decorative imagery— Merce Cunningham and Paul Taylor for example. Which does not mean that a program of elegant gymnastics is all they have to offer to the impresario of a dance theatre. Possibly the most important quality of the American Modern dancer born in the twenties and early thirties is his versatility. As a performer Paul Taylor danced with the Merce Cunningham Company at Black Mountain College in North Carolina and in New York City. He was general male understudy in the Graham Company in '53, toured colleges and appeared with the Pearl Lang Company at Jacob's Pillow then under Ted Shawn's direction. In '58 he was soloist with Martha Graham and created the major role of Aegisthus in her evening-long *Clytemnestra,* a dance version of Aeschylus' *The House of Atreus.* He joined Graham to dance the role of Tiresias in *Night Journey,* the retelling of the Oedipus legend, in Israel, and later on film. And as though that were not enough to demonstrate his mastery of a wide range of techniques he danced a solo choreographed by George Balanchine in the New York City Ballet's *Episodes* (music by Webern), a one-time collaboration between their eminences Graham and Balanchine, the first lord and lady of theatre dance in America.

The dance critic of the *Christian Science Monitor* wrote of Taylor's performance in *Episodes:* "Although his solo was choreographed by the master of balletic adventuring, Mr. Taylor made it so much his own it could have been choreographed by himself. For range, dexterity, quips and quirks and odd transitions, it could hardly have been excelled." The New York City Ballet has given further performances of *Episodes* but Taylor's solo was omitted.

In the early sixties Taylor was again dancing major roles in classic tragedies choreographed by Martha Graham. He played Hercules in *Alcestis* and Theseus in *Phaedra,* while creating and performing (with a small group) works of satire in a contemporary idiom as sharp as that of Aristophanes. None sharper than *Epic,* a solo, set to the voice of a telephone operator in which Taylor in a business suit did very little moving. *Epic,* a full evening work, was first performed at the 92nd Street Y.

In a comment to an interviewer from the *Manchester Guardian* about his choreography Taylor said: "At the beginning, the big New York critics avoided me—they never wrote a line—at that time my audiences were mostly beatniks."

Beatniks—and the student population of the sixties here and abroad—had no trouble understanding Paul Taylor's biting satire of "a consumer society." His sardonic caricatures of industrialized, mechanized urban man delighted the revolutionaries in beads and jeans. Beatnik composers were attacking the establishment (the military-industrial elite) with the thunder of acid rock, the beat writers inspired by Jack Kerouac made poetry out of street argot, the beatnik artists' decor was psychedelic delirium. None of them hit home as hard as the live caricature of the comedian-dancer whose satires of a rotting society and the revolution that toppled it were performed in YM associations, college and university halls, off-Broadway buildings, international dance festivals, and conservative London.

TAYLOR BALLETS

"The Paul Taylor Phenomenon" is the title of a critique published in the French newspaper *Combat* at the time of the International Theatre Festival in Paris, April '62. Taylor won the first prize for choreography. What seemed phenomenal to the French dance critic was not so much the similarity between the fresh content of Taylor's ballet *Junction* and the similarity between Taylor's ballets and the "delicious, surreal innovations" of the Dada insurgent movement that had challenged bourgeois art in France fifty years earlier, as the physical beauty of the six American dancers,* their "animal grace" and flawless muscular coordination.

Peter Lennon, critic for the *Manchester Guardian,* wrote about *Junction* in April '62: "I do not know how much Mr. Taylor owes to his teacher, Martha Graham, or to Balanchine with whom he has danced, but to me his work looked as self-contained as folk dancing, and although steeped, as could be expected, in modern neuroses, it retains the simplicity, purity, and charm of folk dancing." Mr. Lennon was also impressed by the "unflustered originality" of the six young American dancers "who drift out on to the stage with the calmness of respectable Indian chiefs, and go through their gyrations without showing any obvious signs of competing with any tradition."

Back home after the solid accomplishment at the International Theatre Festival Taylor went right on choreographing and dancing in new ballets.

Four months after the International Theatre Festival Taylor and his company performed *Aureole,* a modern dance version of the classic "white" ballet, at the 15th Connecticut Dance Festival, August '62. This "straight" dance work by five barefoot dancers including Paul was an instant success with critics and both right- and left-wing audiences. In '63 the Connecticut Festival commissioned Taylor's *Scudorama.* "It has to do with quickness; like sails or clouds on a windy day" (Doris Hering). "A bitter commentary on the aimless actions of the lost, the insecure, the empty, the terrified and the purposeless" (Walter Terry). Allen Hughes called it "a representative example of dance theatre of the absurd."

Taylor had this to say about *Scudorama:* "It's less concerned

* Elizabeth Walton, Dan Wagoner, Betty De Jong, Shareen Blair, Bonnie Mathis.

with style than a slightly vulgar look. The nasty things the dancers do are related in my mind. . . . to Dante's 'Inferno' which he wrote in the coarse vernacular, rather than his 'Paradiso' which he wrote in a loftier manner. It is a dance that includes uncouth gesture in its movement vocabulary."

Like Alvin Ailey, Merce Cunningham, and others, Taylor was invited to take part in a television repertoire workshop. But the little screen did not render, did not give the feeling of flesh and blood movement, and the program was dropped.

In July 1964, *The Red Room,* a Taylor ballet to the music of Gunther Schuller commissioned by the Festival of Two Worlds, was performed at Spoleto. In August of that year it had its American premiere at the Long Island Arts Festival held on the C. W. Post College campus, Brookville. Allen Hughes wrote in the *New York Times*: "On first sight, this work does not appear to be one of Mr. Taylor's most engrossing choreographic essays. As usual, he has discovered fresh movements to include in his already rich vocabulary, but it is only toward the end of the piece that the materials seem to coalesce into a choregraphic entity. Too much of the time in the early part of the work, there was an awareness that dancing and music were going on simultaneously, that neither had anything to do with the other. . . ." *The Red Room* was later reworked and retitled *Post Meridian* (1965).

A list of Paul Taylor's major works would include *Three Epitaphs,* which was first performed at the Masters Institute in New York and then on May 30, 1954 at the Henry St. Playhouse. This ballet was set to music by the Laneville-Johnson Union Band. It was included in the program presented at the International Theatre Festival, Paris, 1962, along with *Junction, Tablets, Tracer, Insects and Heroes.* There followed *Aureole* (1962), *Scudorama* (1963), *The Red Room* (1964), *Duet* (1964), *Orbs* (1966), *The Book of Beasts* (1971), *Big Bertha* (1971), *American Genesis* (1974), and *Esplanade* (1975) —without Taylor.

Few American Modern dancers from '54 to '75 have had Paul Taylor's range as a choreographer. He was at home in the lyric form, in low comedy, in satire, in nonsense. He moved out of "schools of the dance"—classic, modern, what have you—into theatre. He created "acts" or "numbers" performed by five or six artists on an international music hall circuit. Then, in '75 he stopped dancing.

Will his dance works enter the repertoire of major ballet and dance companies? Or will they fade without his presence?

"He has remarkable grace and a soft fluidity that can reduce modern or ballet technique to silly putty and his group is a superb foil for him." Frances Herridge said that about Paul Taylor in '70. In '75, after he had stopped dancing, she remarked that his group was well trained in his *individual* style but that none of the males could achieve the rubber-jointed sinuousness that had made him unique.

Paul Taylor, by all accounts including his own, chose to put his talent for choreography to work for his talent (genius) as a dancer. A very American choice? Perhaps, and not without a certain endearing, youthful quality. But a choice is a choice and there are consequences. Can anyone rightly claim that what is essentially American folk dance, deserves attention as a classic or universal idiom?

CHAPTER XII

ELIOT FELD AT THE PUBLIC THEATRE
NUREYEV ON BROADWAY

In October '75 Eliot Feld was quizzed by a radio interviewer as his company began a six-week season at Joseph Papp's Public Theatre on Lafayette Street, a short walk south from the site of Tony Pastor's first opera house.

The interviewer asked Eliot Feld what he looked for in a dancer, and what his aims were as a choreographer. The answers: "I look for physical beauty in a dancer," said Eliot Feld. "My choreography tries to express a work of music, to pull out the gut of music into dance."

Further along in the interview he said he rejected acrobatics, percussion movement, fall and recovery, and techniques dear to physical education majors. He was announcing a 180-degree change from the aims and the style of the long-woolens era of American Modern Dance, from dramatic pantomime and character comedy, from witty satire and comic cartoon.

Could it be that American theatrical dancing in the 1970s had come up with a native choreographer who liked Fokine? Feld was not trained at the Maryinsky but he did pick up some classic ballet discipline in New York City, as well as training in musical comedy.

At eleven he began the study of ballet at George Balanchine's School of American Ballet. He danced the role of the child prince in the New York City Ballet's *Nutcracker* that same year.

Eliot could sing as well as dance and at twelve he sang and danced in *Sandhog*, a musical produced by the Phoenix Theatre, also that same year he performed on the "Voice of Firestone." He danced that same year with the Pearl Lang, Sophie Maslow,

159

Mary Anthony, and Donald McKayle companies and was a member of the cast of Ravel's and Colette's *L'Enfant et les Sortileges* produced by the Little Orchestra Society.

A child prodigy? Yes, like the boy of twelve, Tony Pastor, who sang popular ballads on and off the Bowery, entertained the family trade and grew up to father American vaudeville.

Eliot Feld attended the New York High School of Performing Arts, and at sixteen on a dare from his girl tried out for the chorus in the Broadway production of *West Side Story*. He made it. Reviewing his training, could any lessons at the High School for Performing Arts have taught him as much as performing in a Broadway musical under the direction of Jerome Robbins?

Six years later, Eliot was then twenty-two, he joined the American Ballet Theatre. He was promoted to soloist in 1965 and choreographed a ballet for the company in 1967. The ballet was called *Harbinger*, appropriately enough. It was set to Serge Prokoviev's *Concerto #5 for Piano and Orchestra*. Feld danced in it himself, a pas de deux with Christine Sarry, the gamine soubrette who had performed in Agnes de Mille's *Rodeo*. The next day a delirious dance critic saluted "the greatest choreographic find since Jerome Robbins." Eight years and some twenty ballets after that "historic event" Clive Barnes revised the delirious estimate. "Too many people," he wrote, "glibly compare Mr. Feld with Jerome Robbins, forgetting the mutual influence Mr. Tudor exercised on both of them."

It's hard to find much likeness between *Harbinger, At Midnight*, set to music by Mahler, *Songs and Early Songs* (1970) set to Richard Strauss's lieder, and any Robbins or Tudor ballet. Robbins's dancers create character as they move—whether to the music of Bernstein, Chopin, Morton Gould, Stravinsky, Ravel, or to no music at all. Anthony Tudor is a master of dramatic pantomime ballet. Feld's dancers in his own words "pull out the gut of the music" and share it with one another and the audience —you get a little high at a performance of one of Feld's lyric works and most of his works are lyric ensemble ballets.

If some tradition need to be found to explain Feld perhaps Fokine's fourth rule would serve to describe a lyric flow that is so welcome after a decade of satire, abstract expressionism, and psychological probing.

The fourth rule, printed in a letter to the *London Times,* July 1914, that describes the principles of Fokine's choreography is about "the expressiveness of groups and ensemble dancing. . . . The principle of expressiveness advances from the expressiveness of the face, to the expressiveness of the whole body, and from the expressiveness of the whole body, and from the expression of the individual body to the expression of a group of bodies."

There is instant identification between the performers of *Intermezzo,* set to music by Brahms (perhaps everybody's favorite Feld ballet according to Anna Kisselgoff), the performance of the heart-wrenching *Mazurka* (Chopin), and Feld ballet audiences because emotion sensed by the music is expressed by the faces, bodies, and movement of the dancers not shaped into lines or signs, dynamics, or geometry.

Eliot Feld left Lucia Chase's ballet company shortly after the explosion of *Harbinger* and *At Midnight.* There was not, there could not be, instant advancement over everyone's schedule in an established company. Trying out his own wings was a hard and valuable experience for Eliot Feld. But good, even great notices (he was more fortunate in that than Merce Cunningham had been) do not guarantee the immediate appearance of a prestigious patron. The American Ballet Company created with much bravura in 1968 was disbanded in 1970. There had been performances at the Brooklyn Academy of Music, more excellent notices for more excellent ballets (twelve in all) but not enough earning power or financial aid to pay the bills of a ballet company. Eliot survived the loss of his company. He kept right on creating ballets: for the American Ballet Theatre, for the Joffrey Ballet, the Royal Danish Ballet, the National Ballet of Canada, the Royal Swedish Ballet, and the Royal Winnipeg Ballet.

Clearly this is a choreographer who can "write" a widely accepted language, not just a dialect or an elite ritual code for temple or chapel celebrants! Not that he can't turn out a specialty number like *Tzaddik, Sephardic Song, The Real McCoy, Excursion,* but Eliot Feld is first of all master of a lyric vocabulary in ensemble (chorus) dancing that blends folk, court, and ballroom (social) styles. What other art form does this, now? Certainly not architecture, sculpture, painting, rock music, or the movies.

In 1974, with the help of the Rockefeller Foundation, Feld put together another company. He called it the Eliot Feld Ballet and it performed in the three hundred-seat Newman Theatre, at Joseph Papp's Public Playhouse in New York. For a while Lawrence Rhodes was the company's premier danseur. Clive Barnes, who knows about premier danseurs as well and probably better than any newspaper dance critic in the United States, said and says that Lawrence Rhodes is America's only classic first dancer. But Rhodes did not stay long with the Eliot Feld Ballet. He returned to the Pennsylvania Ballet, his home company, before the fall of '75 six-week season at the Newman Theatre. A first dancer in the classic discipline is not a character dancer, not an ensemble dancer. Ensemble dancing is what Feld shows us now. Perhaps he will add a classic ballet to his repertoire. For the present he is not creating any roles for the many great premier danseurs around, Nureyev, Baryshnikov, Bujones, and the American who shows such bright promise, Lawrence Rhodes.

Feld is described by the newsweekly *Time*'s dance critic as having entered the golden circle of United States classic choreographers. "Only Balanchine and Robbins stand ahead of him."

But is it possible to compare Balanchine's Petipa basic training grafted on geometry, Robbins's genius for comedy in movement and character dancing, and Feld's flair for blending the folk rhythm of American Modern Dance and the court dances of Europe? Why not admire each one for his particular quality?

NUREYEV AS AMERICAN HERO

When Martha Graham announced her December 1975 New York season at the Mark Hellinger Theatre, of very special interest were three gala performances entitled:

    I   Opening Night   (December 8)
    II   Americana Evening   (December 16)
    III *The Scarlet Letter*   (December 22).

Brochures and newspaper advertisements informed the public that Martha Graham would appear as onstage commentator at each gala performance and that the Martha Graham Dance Company, its production fund, and the Martha Graham School would benefit from the earnings of the three gala evenings.

The programs of each gala were listed and the names of two dancers. One dancer, Pearl Lang, would appear on the Americana evening in *Letter to the World*. The other, Rudolf Nureyev, would dance *Lucifer* on opening night, the Preacher in *Appalachian Spring* on the Americana evening, and create the role of

Dimmesdale in Martha Graham's version of Nathaniel Hawthorne's *The Scarlet Letter* on December 22.

In the original version of *Appalachian Spring* the principal male roles were created by Merce Cunningham and Erick Hawkins. Merce danced the Preacher, Erick the Husband.

In *Appalachian Spring,* a formidable rival, the American folk hero, will be waiting in the wings for Nureyev's entrance. And again, in the *Scarlet Letter,* when he comes to stand next to Hester Prynne to confess his guilt before the men and women of Puritan Salem, Massachusetts.

One wishes him well. It is of course just possible that a great classic dancer like Nureyev will find some universal quality, a so far unrevealed passion in the American hero that Cunningham, Hawkins, and Paul Taylor have overlooked, something more than a loose-limbed, elastic, animal grace, an impersonal gravity and a dry, wry humor that cuts people and things down to size— the way Will Rogers did.

The premiere of *Lucifer* June 19, 1975, capes by Halston and dance legions of the night by Graham recreated a Denishawn spectacular in which the Russian star crawled, rolled, contracted, expanded, fell and recovered as required. He did all that without condescension—but also without too much emphasis. It was an interesting variation—not the climax of a three-act ballet, not heaven forbid the Rose adagio.

PART II

RUSSIAN BALLET

CHAPTER I

"BALLET DANCING COULD HAVE
A MEANING"

The director of the Imperial Theatres of Russia, Prince Serge
Wolkonsky, "a vigorous young man instead of the usual courtier
or antiquated bureaucrat," said in 1900:

"I do not want you to think of me as a confirmed balletomane
from the start. . . . The first time I went to the ballet it was to see
The Fisherman and the Naiad. . . . I liked the fairy side of the
performance, I liked the corps de ballet but, frankly, I disliked
the soloists. Even in those early days I felt shocked at their affecta-
tion, and the technique, which was stressed to an almost acrobatic
extent, left me quite cold. I could neither grasp the difficulty nor
the charm of it, so tremendously did the 'untruth' of it offend me.
It was true to no convention, illogical, absurd, unnecessary. You
will understand something of it when you compare early theatrical photos with those of today. Then Zucchi came to me as a
great exception and a great revelation. I saw that ballet dancing
could have a 'meaning.' She was one of the greatest mimes I have
ever seen. Everything about her seemed to speak—eyes, shoulders,
hands, and fingers. I shall never forget her lovely expressive back,
when she turned it to the public."

Wolkonsky then describes an "indifferent ballet" called
Brahma, in which Zucchi made the audience cry in spite of bad
music, a dull story and duller décor; her miming was so great
that it conquered the mood of an audience

". . . who had come to see—not art, but physical prowess and
tricks! What was important was the fact that her movements, in
their preparation and in their climax, fell in time to the music.
That may seem obvious now but in those days, music and movement were very far apart. . . .

165

"I remember at the very beginning of my directorship a new production of Tannhäuser. The dances in the first act had been staged by the great Petipa himself. At the dress rehearsal I was horrified. It was just 'tip-toe-tip-toe' the whole time.

"The nymphs were *ballerinas*, never forgot it themselves and never let the audience forget it."

Wolkonsky gave orders for the scene to be changed but, even if there had been time, nobody would have understood what Wolkonsky wanted. In the whole Imperial dancing school there was not even a class of mime. There was a choral singing class but none in musical appreciation. Wolkonsky instituted a mime class under Gert, but he was too academic to give his pupils anything.

"It was only with Fokine, in *Schéhérazade*, in particular, that I saw the practical realization of my dreams."

Wolkonsky was accused of heresy, of wishing to exchange the ballet technique for Dalcroze Eurythmics. Actors, dancers, society, and especially the press were in close alliance "against the director." But just as Isadora Duncan and Ruth St. Denis and Ted Shawn outlived and silenced a hostile press and public in the United States to whom dancing was either bouncing or an attitude, Wolkonsky reformed the Russian stage and paved the way for uniting in Russian Ballet the greatest qualities of Europe—Italian virtuosity, French elegance, Russian feeling.

That Russian and American dancers first came together to share in a cultural understanding, was the result of the vision and pioneering of a Californian, a girl from New Jersey, a young man from Colorado and Prince Serge Wolkonsky, an *enfant terrible* of the Russian theatre.

In appointing his staff assistants, Wolkonsky chose Diaghileff for the "special mission" of producing the *Imperial Theatres Year Book,* an official annual publication. The appointment was an evidence of Wolkonsky's vision, courage and honesty.

Diaghileff was unquestionably qualified for the work expected of him. He had come to St. Petersburg, a country cousin, from Perm, had risen by his own diligence to the leadership of the fashionable aristocratic intelligentsia, swallowing his discomfiture at Rimsky-Korsakoff's pronouncement that he was unworthy to follow a musical career. He had turned to contemporary painting, made friends with artists, and had come into close contact with Benois and Bakst. Visits to Moscow had given him an understanding of the strong nationalist feeling that had swept through that city. Moscow reacted against the Europeanization of Russia, so traditionally the basic creed of St. Petersburg.

Diaghileff had not taken sides with either city. He had made friends with the Moscow merchant patron of the arts, Sava Mamontoff, and the group of young easel painters Mamontoff had engaged to design costumes and scenery for the Russian operas *Boris Godounov, Khovantchina, Sadko,* and *Snegouroutcha,* and Rimsky-Korsakoff's *Pskovitaine,* later re-named *Ivan the Terrible.* He gained much from his association with Mamontoff and Vroubel, "the most versatile artist that Russia has yet produced" and whose décors for the Mamontoff opera pioneered in a direction Bakst was to follow.

The exhibitions of paintings organized and promoted by the country cousin from Perm, united the artistic youth of both capitals and paved the way for the magazine *Mir Isskustva* (The World of Art), a review of which Diaghileff was editor-in-chief, and whose policy was "art for art's sake."

But the very traits of character that had made him triumph over the elegant salon dilettantes of St. Petersburg and enlist the sympathy of the Moscow theatrical arts circle, offended or embarrassed the administrators of a long-established and official institution. His energy, in conflict with the slow procedure of bureaus and their hierarchy, wasted itself in arrogant attitudes. His zeal betrayed him into extravagance. His reckless disregard of financial sobriety (he exceeded the allowance assigned him for the production of the *Imperial Theatres Year Book*) was a bravura gesture neither sound nor politic; it proved that those who called him a show-off and an exhibitionist were right.

The actual cost of the year book was thirty thousand rubles (fifteen thousand dollars), over five thousand dollars in excess of the allotted sum.

It was, however, a most admirable piece of work. The cover and various tailpieces were by Leon Bakst. Benois contributed a learned and profusely illustrated article on the architecture of the Alexandrovsky Theatre. Reproductions of historical portraits were published parallel with the photographs of the actors and actresses who played the roles in the current repertoire which was catalogued and described in the second part of the book together with the personnel and staff of the Imperial Theatre. The essential facts reported about the ballet of the Maryinsky Theatre in the year 1899-1900 were that fifty-five performances were given, that the repertoire included twenty-six ballets, of which four were new works, the most outstanding of which was *The Seasons* by Glazounov. Petipa was on the list of choreographers for the forty-third year and "nearly the whole repertoire is by him. Fokine is emerging. Kchessinka reigns supreme as prima ballerina. Her famous ballet *Esmeralda* was revived with her pet goat in the cast. Anna Pavlowa is beginning to make a name for herself."

As a result of the association with the *Mir Isskustva* group, a new artist was brought in to assist with the production of Rimsky-Korsakoff's opera *Sadko*. The opera was a great success and a great triumph for Wolkonsky as well as for the composer whose work had not been favored by Alexander II and had previously fared badly at the Maryinsky Theatre. In recognition of the help he had received from Diaghileff in connection with *Sadko*, Wolkonsky gave the order that the production of the ballet *Sylvia* be assigned to him. But on the eve of the official announcement of this appointment, a general strike by the many who had been offended by Diaghileff's manners and morals, forced Wolkonsky to rescind the order.

Relations between the *Mir Isskustva* group and the Imperial Theatre came to an end. The first looked west; the second, after the dismissal of Wolkonsky, was put under the direction of Teliakovsky, an ancient guard officer who, although aesthetically uninspired, was rugged enough to hold his own in political intrigues and carry out his predecessor's ideas.

Diaghileff waited for Teliakovsky to fall. But as the guard officer survived the Revolution of 1905 and emerged from the conflict stronger than ever with Fokine a rising star, Diaghileff turned to Paris. In 1906, he organized the Russian Exhibition at the Salon d'Automne, in the Grand Palais. The exhibition filled twelve rooms and contained 750 items borrowed from the

Imperial Palaces, museums and private collections. Diaghileff had begun his career as promoter of Russian art in Europe.

The exhibition was a sensational success. It presented the contemporary Russian artist to a delighted French public. It also presented Mr. Diaghileff to the western public in the light of an extremely able organizer. From then on, the French with their genius for clarity never described him in any other way than as *l'animateur,* a word for which there is no exact equivalent in English.

After showing Russian painting to Paris, the idea of a series of historic concerts came as a matter of course, and in 1907 Diaghileff presented a series of "historic concerts" at the Paris Opera House that popularized Russian music as a whole for a long time. To be sure, the French musicians (Debussy, among others) were acquainted with the works of Moussorgsky and Rimsky-Korsakoff, but Tchaikovsky was considered "trivial and vulgar." Walter Nouvel wrote of this:

"It was in vain that I told them that we considered him (Tchaikovsky) the most national of our composers, that he alone knew how to render the soul of the Russian nineteenth century . . . all my eloquence was in vain, and what amazed me still more was the fact that they were unwilling to admit even his purely musical gifts, his technique, his sense of rhythm, and the mastery of his orchestration."

The "historic concerts" were received with as much enthusiasm as the exhibition of Russian painting had been. The program was ambitious and costly. Whole acts of operas and concertos by Glazounov, Rachmaninov, Rimsky-Korsakoff, Borodine, Scriabine and Glinka were to be performed with the composers conducting or performing their works and the foremost singers of the St. Petersburg and Moscow operas, led by Chaliapin, appearing in their most famous roles.

For the sake of conciliating the French, Tchaikovsky was omitted. The critic of the *Figaro* took charge of the publicity; the Comtesse de Greffulhe, president of the Grandes Auditions de France, supplied the indispensable social contacts; and Giles van de Pals, "a rich St. Petersburg music lover," the even more indispensable sum of ten thousand rubles.

Moussorgsky made the greatest success of any of the composers; Chaliapin received an ovation when he sang Galitzky's song from *Prince Igor*. Diaghileff immediately saw his next move. His dream of producing a mammoth theatrical spectacle would be realized. He would stage *Boris Godounov* at the Paris Opera.

The Diaghileff production of *Boris Godounov* not only showed the Parisians "a work of genius, the best resources of the Russian theatre, and décor and production undreamed of in the West," it also encouraged the man who had pleased the most capricious audience in the world three times in succession to "try it again" . . . this time with ballet.

Many years later, when asked about the origin of his Russian Ballet in Western Europe, Daighileff answered, "I had already presented Russain painting, Russian music, and Russian opera in Paris, and from opera to ballet was but a step. Ballet contained in itself all these other activities."

Diaghileff planned his season of ballet and opera at the Theatre du Châtelet, in Paris, immediately after the close of *Boris*. The entire enterprise was built around Fokine and Nijinsky, the latter because it was Diaghileff's avowed purpose to "give the French audience an idea of what a male dancer can be." The French art of dancing was ballerina ridden.

The repertoire included four ballets* with choreography by Fokine, the first act of *Rousslan and Ludmila* and an abbreviated version of *Ivan the Terrible*, one of Chaliapin's greatest roles.

The company of fifty-five dancers was headed by Anna Pavlowa who had already had the experience of leaving the Imperial Ballet for a tour under the direction of Adolf Bolm, in which performances were given at Helsingfors, Stockholm, Copenhagen, and Prague and, early in 1909, Berlin.

The leading male dancers were Nijinsky and Mordkin; the corps was as evenly divided as possible between the Moscow and the St. Petersburg schools. Karsavina, Ida Rubinstein, Theodore Koslov, and Adolf Bolm were supporting artists. Without any doubt, it was the greatest show of Russian Ballet on earth. But no provision had been made by its showman to pay for it.

---

* *Le Pavillon d'Armide, Cleopatre, Les Sylphides* (produced in Russia as *Chopiniana*), and *Le Festin* (a divertissement on a large scale).

No state subvention was likely, so Diaghileff, according to the curious explanation of Arnold Haskell, devised a scheme that while

". . . morally indefensible, was *almost* excusable, since not a penny was to be diverted to his own uses and no one was in any way harmed by it.

"In Russia there was a law that said that the heads of commercial houses established for over a hundred years could apply for hereditary patents of nobility. They could apply, but that did not mean their applications would be granted without much influence and pressure from the powerful. A certain Mr. K., the head of a rubber manufactory, was devoured by such ambitions, and proposed to pay Diaghileff the sum of ten thousand pounds if his Grand Ducal patron would endorse the application. The Grand Duke . . . was easily persuaded, and the whole matter seemed on the point of accomplishment when he died without having written the letter."*

Heartbroken, Diaghileff came sobbing to his friends. The Grand Duchess did not share her husband's regard for Diaghileff. She had no interest in the production of Russian Ballet abroad. Everything was at a standstill.

Arnold Haskell concluded his account of this incident with the following sentence:

"Fortunately, at the last minute, through other influences, the scheme went through, Mr. K. became a noble, and Western Europe was able to see the Russian Ballet. . . . On such ambitions does the fate of great enterprises sometimes rest."

The season of Russian Ballet and opera was a success. Accounts of it appear in every social and artistic memoir of the period. The figures of the receipts were astronomical but, as usual, Diaghileff had spent recklessly and in spite of the help of the wealthy men of Paris, there remained a deficit of sixty thousand francs, and Diaghileff left his headquarters heavily in debt.

From then on, for twenty years, the story of this impresario repeats itself. A nomad, he lived at the Grand Hotel in Paris, the Savoy in London, the Hotel de Paris in Monte Carlo, hotels in Lido and Venice, arranging for "next year's season of ballet," begging, borrowing and squandering money.

* From Arnold Haskell's *Life of Diaghileff*.

If Paris can be said to have been the Broadway of Europe from 1909 to 1929, then the Diaghileff Ballet may be called its Ziegfeld Follies. Both theatres discovered and made great stars, employed the finest talents in dance, décor, miming and music. Fokine created ballets for Ziegfeld, one to music by Victor Herbert. Both expressed the splendor of a dying empire—a feverish, sumptuous, spectacular finale.

The reception of the 1909 program in Paris affected the whole subsequent history of ballet. The French audiences were discriminating, and very definite about what they did and did not like. Anna Pavlowa was not a success. The Parisian preferred Ida Rubinstein, whose frankly sensuous appeal in *Cleopatre* had much the same magic as Ruth St. Denis' *Radha* without Miss St. Denis' transcendental pretension.

Le Pavillon d'Armide, which was set in the France of Louis XIV, was a failure. The French expected something "exotic" from the Russians, not an interpretation of their own Golden Age. For the same reason they were not enthusiastic about *Les Sylphides.* A *ballet blanc* based on a scenario written by Theophile Gautier? Why had the Russians chosen such a subject? The real success of the season was *Prince Igor.* Here was a thrill. "The real air of the steppes, the wild Asiatic horde, real male dancing; a corps de ballet that was more than a piece of scenery." Nijinsky and Bolm were acclaimed. Ballerinas were no novelty in Paris, but great male dancers and a fine ensemble were.

At the end of the season, Pavlowa left. Spessivtseva took her place and to the end of their lives, Diaghileff and the great Russian ballerina were never entirely reconciled. Diaghileff once said of Anna Pavlowa, "She was never really interested in art as such. The only thing that mattered to her was her own virtuosity, and she is a virtuoso without equal."

CHAPTER II

RUSSIAN BALLET IN THE UNITED STATES

Russian painting and Russian music introduced Russian Ballet in Western Europe. But in the United States, no museum and no program of "historic concerts" could have roused popular interest in the work of Russian painters and composers. We were not very much alive to painting and "classical music" in 1909. These subjects were reserved for intellectuals and the women's clubs.

Our popular theatre was vaudeville, burlesque, operetta, and the review with music. If we had developed no outstanding dramatist, our tragedians such as Edwin Booth could play Shakespeare with distinction; our clowns were to make our moving picture something more than a beauty contest, and as a people we liked to dance and to see good dancing. It was not by accident that we came by an artist like Isadora Duncan.

Nor was it by accident that Russian Ballet by Pavlowa and Mordkin was "a milestone in the history of ballet in America." The two dancers who had left the Diaghileff forces after its 1909 season in Paris, succeeded in their first and subsequent performances in America because as soloists they combined beauty, strength, technique and the ability to evoke poetic imagery.

Pavlowa was a beautiful woman, a classic dancer, and as sensitive to overtones as any poet. Mordkin, whom the American press promptly described as a Greek god, seemed some figure from the Parthenon marbles. After one season at the Metropolitan in New York in the spring of 1910, Pavlowa and Mordkin were commissioned by the Metropolitan to return the following autumn with a company engaged by them in Russia. The project included a single initial appearance in New York, and a trip to the Pacific Coast with a return engagement in New York when the season was at its height.

To their first program, which had included *Coppelia, Hungary,*

173

and *Autumn Bacchanale,* a dance filched from Fokine's ballet *Cleopatre,* were added for the fall season of 1910: *Giselle, The Legend of Aziade,* and a number of divertissements, the most famous of which was *The Dying Swan,* which Fokine had created for Pavlowa in 1905. The historical note about this dance, written by Cyril W. Beaumont, seems worth quoting:

"Enthusiastic over the possibilities of ballet reform, Fokine composed a letter which he sent to various artistes asking them to favor him with their views on ballet. What did they understand by ballet? Some artists did not trouble to reply, while others appeared to hold no particular views on the subject.

"It is not difficult to realize the extent of Fokine's disappointment when he found that not only did the general public refuse to take the ballet seriously, but even the artists themselves appeared to regard it purely as a means of existence. He began to wonder whether it was worth while to devote his life to an art held in such little honor. . . . Nevertheless, Fokine felt so strongly the possibility of speedy success and of being able to reform the ballet that he decided to continue.

"The same year was marked by the production of the dance now known all over the world as *Le Cygne (The Dying Swan).* Anna Pavlowa visited a rehearsal room where Fokine was teaching and asked him to arrange a dance for her. She had promised to appear at a concert to be given at the Hall of Assembly of Noblemen by the artists of the chorus of the Imperial Russian Opera.

"Fokine consented and then considered what form the dance should take. He mused on the dancer's long and graceful neck, the softness of her line, and felt that the dance should be beautiful, lyric, and expressive. *Le Cygne* was born from those thoughts.

"Not only is this dance one of Fokine's most beautiful and poetic creations, but it illustrates to the full his conception of the art of ballet, *while based on the traditional costume and technique of the old ballet.*

"This dance demands from the dancer a high standard of technique, which is not, however, used *to astonish but to create a poetic image.*"

In other words, this dance was not athletic nor spectacular divertissement. It was poetic motion and imagery.

The tour to the Pacific Coast was an echo of the success of Russian Ballet by Pavlowa and Mordkin at the Metropolitan Opera House in New York City. Smaller towns approved of the "ballet dancer unequalled by any save one* in our generation who is also a genuine actress!" *The Argonaut* in San Francisco wrote:

"The set smile of the ballet is not for her. Entreaty, coquetry, passion, fear, terror, even madness and the simulated convulsions of approaching death are all equally at her command. She is young, slender and symmetrical, and endowed with a beauty that gives a peculiar charm to her dramatic expression."

The same paper wrote of Mordkin:

"He is physically fit to be a sculptor's model, *and thought and emotion as well as manly beauty mark his face."* [The italics are the writer's.]

Frederick King, editor of the *Literary Digest,* remarked that one thing Mordkin may be said to have done for our audiences was to make the male dancer acceptable. At this time (1911) Ted Shawn was only twenty. It is likely Mr. King did not know Shawn had been sent on tour by the Santa Fé Railroad to dance *historic dances* in the Santa Fé vacation camps for employees.

Shawn's comments about Pavlowa pay tribute to him as well as to the great ballerina:

"Pavlowa is in the realm of the dance what Paderewski is in the realm of music—a superlative virtuoso. She has the technique, she has the fire, she has the personality to thrill audiences, to satisfy them from the standpoint of sheer power that radiates in her dancing, but so far as I know, she has created nothing. I do not know of one single movement or step that she has added to the vocabulary of the dance. . . . Pavlowa stands exactly as Taglioni . . . and Camargo . . . before her."

Mr. Shawn remarked that Olin Downes' criticism in a New York paper the preceding winter had been written not wisely but too well. Shawn believed that virtuosos have charm and personality, but that it is creators who are the real benefactors to the progress of the dance. He went on to express the opinion that as Raphael changed an entire method of painting and Bach profoundly affected the development of music in his time, Isadora Duncan and Ruth St. Denis would take their place as creative geniuses who gave a new direction to the art of the dance.

* Adeline Genée.

In 1911, while the Russian stars were touring the United States, Ruth St. Denis was doing the same in *Radha*. In the same year, too, Isadora Duncan was dancing Bach-Wagner programs accompanied by a symphony orchestra led by Walter Damrosch.

It is difficult to evaluate the comparative popularity of these great artists. The fairest judgment seems to be that Russian Ballet had taken root in America. The American manager was alert to the new taste and prompt to cater to it in his own interest.

In September, 1910, a group headed by Victorina Galemberti, première danseuse at the Manhattan Opera House, and her partner, Giovanni Molassi, announced a program of *"Danses Classiques Russes,* the dancing sensation of the season as presented at the Imperial Opera of St. Petersburg." These dances were presented at the American Music Hall, an auditorium that stood on the corner of Eighth Avenue and Forty-second Street. Although the supporting members of the troupe had names as un-Russian as the stars, the program gave assurance that the scene used was an exact reproduction of the ballet scene of the Imperial Opera. Frederick King remarked that if this were true, as seems probable, there must have been little difference between the ballet scene of the Imperial Opera and that provided by our own theatres. Galemberti and Molassi did an adagio designed to please "the most volatile Italian" when the man in arabesque supported the woman "perched perilously on her back, supported on his hip." Similar scenes were for years a part of our vaudeville fare. The Russian Ballet at the American Music Hall was clearly pre-Fokine.

But one year later, at the Winter Garden in New York, Miss Gertrude Hoffman, a successful vaudeville star herself, having seen the Russian Ballet in Paris, aspired to be the American Diaghileff, and presented a *Saison de Ballets Russes.*

It was a heroic effort. First, because Miss Hoffman had enough courage and sufficient ability to earn all the money to finance the undertaking herself; second, because she had vision enough to produce *Scheherazade, Cleopatre,* and *Sylphides,* although not enough sense of fair play to give Fokine a credit line in the program, and third, because she was able to assemble and manage a company of two hundred recruited from the St. Petersburg and Moscow Ballets.

The director of Gertrude Hoffman's Ballet Russe was Theodore Koslov, who represented the Moscow School. The premier male mime was Alexis Bulgakov from the Imperial Theatre in St. Petersburg. The outstanding ballerina was the charming Lydia Lopoukova, and the title roles in *Cleopatre* and *Schéhérazade* were played by Miss Hoffman herself, who had already become notable for her *Salome* dances.

(It may be noted that the Old Testament had familiarized the American audience with Oriental themes. Egypt and the court of Solomon were part of the American folk idiom; and the colorful dramas of kings, concubines, slaves and dancing girls, learned from church, home or Sunday school, were popular subjects for musical or theatrical treatment.)

Although Miss Hoffman's Winter Garden season, in 1911, was presented in the hottest summer New York had known in over a decade, and on two occasions performances had to be postponed until the weather cooled off, wild enthusiasm ruled among the spectators "who in contrast to opera audiences, represented the popular element to whom ballet meant high kicking."

The bright particular star of Miss Gertrude Hoffman's Ballet Russe was Lydia Lopoukova. The nineteen-year-old Russian girl was hailed as a modern Taglioni, although her opulent charm in no way resembled the ethereal grace of the demure Maria.

The solo dances in *Sylphides* were danced by Lopoukova and Alexis Bulgakov and were frantically acclaimed; the stage sets were attributed to Bakst, although they were only imitations of that artist's work. The New York press comment reported that "such dancing and such stage settings had never before been seen on our stage."

The police, however, became disturbed about the propriety of these ballets and the entire company was hailed into court. Upon testimony of Morris Gest, David Belasco and Prince Nicholas Koudachoff, Charge d'Affaires at the Russian Embassy at Washington, the case was dismissed.

At the close of the Winter Garden engagement, the company moved west. But the success in New York was not repeated in Chicago, Detroit and Vancouver. Not until the Hoffman Ballet Russe reached San Francisco did large audiences offset part of the losses of the tour.

A greater loss than that of a monetary deficit befell Miss Hoffman when Lopoukova and Volinin were "enticed away by a rival manager." The impresario-actress had to revert to her long list of impersonations of reigning stage favorites to fill out the program of what no longer could be called "Ballet Russe."

CHAPTER III

ALL-STAR RUSSIAN IMPERIAL BALLET—MORDKIN

In December, 1911, the Metropolitan Opera House in New York City presented *Le Lac des Cygnes* (*Swan Lake*) with Ekaterina Geltser, Mordkin and Volinin in the principal roles.

The preliminary press notices had announced that, thanks to the gracious dispensation of the Russian government, the most famous ballet organization in the world would have a New York season and a three-year tour of the principal cities of the United States, Canada and Central America under the direction of Max Rabinoff, Inc.

The new ballet was described as "ocular opera." It was "real ballet" as presented by the great Russians, which consisted of mimodrama or the unfolding and enactment of narrative drama.

"Only the graceful movement of the premiers and premières, and the rhythmic sway of the supporting dancers, supplemented by music especially written for the purpose, illuminate the theme or plot. Not a line is spoken, not a word sung. Yet it is all perfectly understandable to Slav or Saxon, Greek or Gaul—to all who have eyes to see—for each story is interpreted in the great universal language, 'the poetry of action.' 'Action' is substituted for 'motion.'"

Ballet Russe with Mordkin at the Metropolitan was, in a word, *ballet d'action* or pantomime.

The repertoire included *Coppelia* and a supplementary list of divertissements. Ballet performances were given Tuesday nights, at which time the Opera did not play. An occasional divertissement was brought out when a short opera permitted. "The divertissement frequently caught the fancy of the audience more than the works of the formal ballet."

Swan Lake was particularly near to Mordkin's heart. He made certain changes in the original Petipa version first produced in 1876, and the first ballet to which Tchaikovsky set the music.

179

It had already been changed by Diaghileff when he revived it in Paris in 1909, at which time the magical element in the old German fairy tale was emphasized by introducing a vision of swans floating lightly on the bosom of a shimmering lake during the orchestral prelude.

The Mordkin version opened in the great hall of the castle of Prince Siegfried and concluded with the death of both the hapless Prince and Odette, the girl transformed by sorcery into a swan, of whom he had become enamored. Geltser, of German descent but Russian born and bred, and eminent in the Moscow ballet where she had often been Mordkin's partner, was a sumptuous beauty and an expert technician in the acrobatic style—the precise opposite of Pavlowa! She executed magnificent dances but when Mordkin left the Imperial Russian Ballet on January 15, 1912, he figured in dancing episodes in a Shubert review called *Vera Violetta* with his wife and Lydia Lopoukova.

Vera Violetta was running at the Winter Garden. In its cast were Al Jolson, Gaby Deslys and her partner, Harry Pilcer, as well as the great Russian dancers. For the first time, Mordkin found his name seconding another. Acton Davies, the outspoken critic of the *Sun*, wrote:

"About which was the great success, there could be no possible shadow of a doubt—it was La Lopoukova. Her wonderful youth, her sinuous grace captivated the audience. . . . Mordkin, to be sure, is an exquisitely beautiful dancer; no one can take that away from him; but . . . on that Winter Garden stage last night, Mordkin for the first time in his career had to stand comparison."

At the close of the Winter Garden engagement, Mordkin returned to Moscow. He enrolled as a reservist in the Russian Army but was permitted to pursue his legitimate career. After many painful experiences, he sought refuge in the Caucasus from 1918 to 1922. To escape an epidemic of typhus, he returned to Moscow where he worked until 1925, at which time Morris Gest sent for him to take part in an American tour that did not include New York. The pieces presented were *Carnaval*, to music by Liszt, *Aziade*, previously presented in America, a rose ballet, and *Melodie Hebraique*. Among the members of the company were Nemchinova, Butsova, formerly of the Pavlowa company, and Pierre Vladimirov.

Reviews in western papers said Nemchinova had a peculiar brilliance which lost nothing by comparison with the greatest dancers the Russian Ballet had brought to America; Vladimirov was credited with youthful fire and spontaneous grace; Mordkin, it was noted, retained his definitely artistic and dramatic expressiveness although "this was now limited to the impressions created by a purely facial intensity, and a skill in posing without highly animated movement."

CHAPTER IV

PAVLOWA AGAIN

STYLE WITHOUT SEX—BOURGEOIS PURITAN

In 1912, Acton Davies, the critic of the *New York Sun,* had remarked that the American public was "fed up" with Russian Ballet.

In 1913, Pavlowa re-appeared at the Metropolitan Opera House with her own company, had a return engagement in 1914, toured the country in 1914-15, and in 1915-16 joined forces with the Boston Opera Company, in which she invested a considerable share of her own means to keep the company from collapse.

But her program was not in any sense true "Russian Ballet." She was too intelligent to give the American public what they neither wanted nor needed; Ruth St. Denis, who was physically more appealing to the great American public than any Russian ballerina, evoked on our stage what Ida Rubinstein did in Paris— a sensual thrill. But Pavlowa knew as well as Miss St. Denis did, that technical competence and style had a public, and she was sensible enough to address herself to that public. It never failed her.

At the Metropolitan in the fall of 1913, she offered *Oriental Fantasies, The Magic Flute, The Pavlowa Gavotte* (which had had its world première in Meriden, Connecticut), and a series of divertissements, among them *Les Preludes,* inspired by Lamartine's *Les Meditations,* with music by Liszt. To this repertoire she later added *Moment Musical* by Schubert, which recalled Isadora Duncan and which became a general favorite, *Autumn Bacchanale, The Swan* and, in her second season, *La Fille Mal Gardée, Paquita,* a suite of classical Spanish dances (a Spanish *Pas de Quatre),* included in the repertoire of the Maryinsky Theatre, *Invitation to the Dance* to Weber's music, *Amarilla,* the gypsy ballet Frederick King calls one of Pavlowa's *tours de force, The Fairy Doll* and *The Seven Daughters of the Ghost King,* the last

182

two by Fokine; also ballets by Ivan Clustine, ballet master of the Paris Opera, after his retirement from the Imperial Russian Theatre.

Clustine was an adherent of the old school. He was very sympathetic toward Pavlowa, who only included Fokine ballets as a bow to the supreme master of the "new trend"; she felt more at home in such works as *Le Reveil de Flora, Walpurgis Night* and *Raymonda,* filched and refurbished from the old Petersburg repertoire by Clustine.

All critics agreed that this repertoire was dowdy in costume, that its decor was frumpy and its musical accompaniment mediocre. The entertainment she provided was neither bold in theme nor of solid structure. It was salon or parlor entertainment; it pleased Victorian conventions.

Pavlowa, "who loved everything German," had broken away from the Italian ballet postures and introduced the Hellenic, according to the German school of classicism (a mixture of Plato, Transcendentalism and flamboyant Gothic). Her movements were harmonious; her effects simple. She was not the greatest technician in her field, but she did certain steps as no other dancer could, in a style that was unsurpassable and, above all, personal—a style that might be called the poetic representation of that caste disparagingly called "bourgeois Puritan" by its rivals and victims.

Her collaboration with the Boston Opera Company was a failure. A great hope had sprung up at the news of her undertaking. Boston music lovers were ready for Russian music, "for operas in which the music was adjusted to the necessities of expression, not the display of technique," as one writer put it. But, alas! how was the dancer to produce the works of Glinka, Cesar Cui, Balakirev, Borodine, Moussorgsky and Rimsky-Korsakoff with Roberto Moranzoni, Agide Jacchia and a cast of Italian singers?

The optimists had forgotten, too, that Pavlowa was notably weak on the side of music; almost anything with a danceable tune and rhythm would do for her. She never hesitated to change a composition to suit her personal needs, altering the time, making cuts and repeats at will. If the orchestra leader demurred, she used to say, "They do not come to hear the music. They come to see Pavlowa dance."

To meet the staggering losses accumulated by her venture into music, drama, and ballet, she gallantly accepted Charles Dillingham's offer to bill her at the Hippodrome, with trained elephants, acrobats, skaters, and clowns, for $8,500 a week.

But the important fact established by her tremendous success at the Hippodrome was overlooked by the would-be Diaghileffs for many years to come, as well as by that gentleman himself when he brought a company to the United States in 1916 without the expected "stars."

Neither Anna Pavlowa nor the American audiences that acclaimed her were as interested in the dance as they were in the dancer. It was not the meaning and the matter of a beautiful or exciting dance composition that filled the Hippodrome twice a day. The *Sleeping Beauty,* a Petipa ballet to the music of Tchaikovsky, refurbished with glittering and bespangled Bakst costumes, had to be dropped! The audience was given a hand at selecting the program and unhesitatingly replaced *Sleeping Beauty* with *Gavotte Pavlowa.*

Russian Ballet. . . . "After me the world will not know it!" Pavlowa is reported to have said that. In the sense that the Imperial Russian Ballet was pure divertissement for the Emperor and his court, she was right. In the larger sense, it must be said that today the vast dance audience of the western world knows the masterpieces of the great Russian choreographers.

CHAPTER V

THE DIAGHILEFF FIASCO

In 1915, the Metropolitan Opera Company needed something to replace its German repertoire. It chose Russian Ballet as the best substitute. The Metropolitan Opera Company, however, was not prepared to undertake the organization and supervision of a Russian Ballet in the United States and a subsidiary company was formed under the name of The Metropolitan Ballet Company. Otto Kahn, whose name did not appear in the prospectus, was understood to be the principal backer of this theatrical venture.

The Diaghileff Company, marooned in Switzerland, was approached. A few matters of "plain" American business were set before Serge Diaghileff. He must have his troupe on hand at such an hour, on such a date, and his scenery must be in the theatre at such a moment. The Russian impresario, who had declared his independence of his native land and was now wandering in exile, flew into an artistic fury.

Unfortunately, he was calmed down before one or two essential pieces of information had been obtained by the representatives of "plain American business." These were the names of the artists Mr. Diaghileff would bring to America, and the titles of the ballets he proposed to produce.

It is hard to understand why Diaghileff was given a contract on the assumption that his company would include Fokine, Nijinsky, and Karsavina. Fokine, whose ballets were primarily based on folklore and fairy story, was working in Russia undisturbed by political conflicts. He was acting as maître de ballet at the Maryinsky Theatre. Karsavina, by her own account, could not and would not leave the country. Vaslav Nijinsky was a virtual prisoner of war in Hungary. Why were these facts not discovered by the Metropolitan Opera Ballet? And why did the advance publicity for the Diaghileff Ballet Russe contain portraits of these stars if the management had not defintiely contracted for their appearance?

185

The answer seems to be that the wealthy men of New York, like the wealthy men of Paris, were not good business men and that Diaghileff was smart enough to take advantage of them. The season he gave at the Century Theatre in New York, on tour and at the Metropolitan Opera House for four weeks in the spring of 1916, was not a success, even though the arrival of Nijinsky on the third of April saved a defeat from becoming a rout.

The New York audiences, most of them acquainted with Paris, were interested if not overwhelmed. Massine did as well as could have been expected with Nijinsky's roles; the orchestra which received praise almost in excess of the dancing under the direction of Ernest Ansermet did well by the great Russian composers. But the brilliant and bizarre scenery designed by Bakst looked "worn with a number of years' usage"; and "the high responsibility laid upon Mme. Maclezova, the prima ballerina, was not met by that lady's gifts of imagination, though little fault was found with her technical equipment."

The only real hit in the repertoire which included Fokine's *Firebird*, to music by Stravinsky, *Schéhérazade*, already familiar through the Winter Garden performances, *Les Sylphides*, *Carnaval*, *Prince Igor*, *Thamar*, *Le Pavillon d'Armide*, Nijinsky's *L'Après Midi d'un Faune*, Massine's *Soleil de Nuit*, and Fokine's *Petrouchka*, was the last named.

"A New York audience, so little blasé as to break into the performance with chuckles of very audible laughter, applauded long and fervently. It was the applause of an enthusiasm which had no room for fault-finding."

The company went from New York to Boston. Boston was fortunate in having a critic like "H.T.P." of the *Transcript*. Before the ballet opened, he wrote long articles describing the nature of the art and its evolution from the stereotyped so-called "classic" form, to the theatrical form in which a skeleton of precision and mechanics was clothed and made alive by the miracle of music, color and pantomime. Parker also reviewed the Diaghileff Ballet as he had observed it in Europe, and prepared Massachusetts for the latest Paris fashion in theatre art.

At the outset, Boston seemed to take the ballet for its own

sake and made no complaint over the absence of first-class soloists. Mmes. Maclezova and Revalles were seen to be dancers of the second rank, but the ensemble conquered. The audiences were small at the beginning, but before the end of the engagement the interest and attendance increased so much that the intervening engagements to play in smaller towns between Boston and Chicago were cancelled, and Boston was given the benefit of additional performances.

The Boston city government, so notoriously alert lest public morals be contaminated by the stage, had its mentor review the performances of *Schéhérazade* and *L'Après Midi d'un Faune*. Nothing was found amiss, however. But being of sharp temper and "liking little to be crossed in its ways," the ballet added a touch of devilment to its last performances—a new miming of the faun, and unsparing vigor in the interpretation of *Schéhérazade*.

In Chicago, critics and audience alike were bewildered. The ballet was supposed to be "caviar." Yet, on opening night the fashionable audience behaved much as it did at a show. One earnest spectator reported, "They talked in the most discourteous way, as though they were witnessing something like a sublimated Follies, in which the orchestra was a negligible quantity and the main interest a pleasurable anticipation of better pornography than ever before. They were disappointed in this respect and they showed it."

The commentator did not seem to notice that Chicago's first night audience had taken the ballet as its creators, the Imperial Romans, had taken it—not as an eclectic and precious court pastime, nor as the solemn expression of a ritual or religion, but as first-rate entertainment, burlesque and horseplay.

The Chicago newspaper critics were not dance-minded. Their regular assignments were the review of music and theatre, which in 1915 meant Beethoven, Brahms, Wagner, Shakespeare and George Bernard Shaw.

It was not strange that they were baffled by Stravinsky's "anarchical dissonances," or resentful of the barbaric carnality of *Schéhérazade*, which was described as "that Ossa upon Pelion, a debauch in a harem," and that they criticized the Faun for its ugly and material conclusion. But their condemnation helped keep people away. The money loss was great. One paper tried to mollify the disappointed backers by publishing the following sentiment on its editorial page:

"Our thin and self-conscious culture prevents any frank and expansive surrender to sheer sensuous beauty. Our motto is safety first and Mrs. Grundy never leaves our elbow."

The Russian Ballet returned to the Metropolitan on April 3. On April 12, Nijinsky made his first appearance, and the ballet began to take on new life.

Ballets in which he danced, bore evidence of his directing skill, and the others gave signs of rejuvenation. A disquieting public apathy was dispelled, and large audiences attended every performance.

Frederick King wrote that critics, especially in America, had been unwilling to grant to the male dancer the attributes of grace and charm although the idea he expressed demanded those qualities. But even such a masculine critic as Henry Krehbiel was forced to yield to the high qualities of Nijinsky. Nijinsky might lack the virility of Mordkin, but as a dancer pure and simple, and as an interpretive artist and original personality, he stood alone.

"His movements flow one from another without effort and without break in a kind of muscular legato . . ."

The success of Nijinsky was a painful experience for the impresario of the company. Diaghileff had resented Nijinsky's marriage and his independent attitude. It was difficult for him to see his own poor record in the United States partially saved by the greatest star in his troupe, and one whom he had alienated.

Nor was Nijinsky's position an altogether enviable one. As the choreographer of *L'Après Midi d'un Faune,* he refused to accept the interpretation of his ballet that Diaghileff had presented. In *Sylphides* and *Carnaval, La Princesse Enchantée, Schéhérazade, Spectre de la Rose* and *Petrouchka,* he outdanced and surpassed everyone.

Not for nothing had Sarah Bernhardt cried out after seeing him dance in Paris, "J'ai peur, j'ai peur car je vois l'alteur le plus grand du monde."

This man, who was the very incarnation of human feeling and emotion, frightened his fellow artists as well as his admirers. His humor, his vigor and his fantasy as Harlequin in *Carnaval,* his poetic quality in *Les Sylphides,* his brilliance and pace in *Spectre de la Rose* and *Scheherazade,* showed that his predecessors, although skillful dancers, were altogether out of his class.

His pace sometimes brought a look of pained apprehension to the face of his partner, Lydia Lopoukova. "To Maclezova it would have spelled ultimate disaster."

His choreographic inventions in *The Faun* and *Sacre du Printemps* and in the short-lived *Jeux* had broken with the romantic tradition. He had replaced the roundness and softness characteristic of the nineteenth century ballet with straight lines, angles and virile tension. This did not prevent his interpreting romantic roles to perfection. There was a lively dispute between the people who claimed Nijinsky's greatest role was in *Spectre,* those who insisted the frenzy of his acting in *Schéhérazade* was his supreme accomplishment, and the purists who never missed a performance of *Les Sylphides* and insisted that his performance of the single male part deserved the highest praise.

One commentator wrote:

"The hesitant yet sure movements of the hands, the utterly graceful poses inspired by a wistfulness of mood, aptly translated the music into visibility; these were quite as wonderful as the most floating movements of the dance."

Another described his whitened face and blond ringlets as accenting the unreality of the perennially favorite ballet in which Nijinsky made the style something after Aubrey Beardsley.

But the American public would not accept any work based on adolescent male idol worship, not even from Nijinsky. The performance of *Narcisse,* Fokine's masterpiece to the music of Tcherepnine with décor by Bakst, which was given at the Metropolitan Opera House on April 29 with Nijinsky in the title role, let loose murmurs about the effeminacy in such a storm that the second performance had to be cancelled.

Narcisse was said to express more than any other ballet the ideals which Fokine had at heart. Cyril Beaumont wrote that this was Benois' opinion, and he quoted the following comment about the first performance of *Narcisse* which took place in Paris in 1911:

"Narcisse obtained a triumphal success shared by the 'maître de ballet,' Fokine, whose dances are admirably arranged, Nijinsky, who surpasses the renown of Vestris, Mmes. Fokina, Nijinska, and finally, the delicious Karsavina in the character of Echo."

In this composition Fokine made no concession to the traditional pseudo-antique style. The corps appeared as wood sprites, Boetian rustics and Bacchantes whose movements and gestures, carefully modelled after Greek sculpture and relief, supplied an admirable background for the severely simple classic movements of Echo and Narcissus. The scenery was designed by Bakst, who had collaborated on the development of the theme with the composer Tcherepnine.

The London reviews were as favorable as those in Paris, with more enthusiasm for the spectacular qualities of the work than its symbolism. The English critics commented on the poetical yet fantastic conception, on the dances that were entirely different from those already seen, more charming, more graceful, with less suggestion of the acrobatic. ". . . And the unsullied joy of the first dances of Narcissus . . . are as captivating as anything the Russians have given us."

Were American audiences affronted by the theme of a young man falling in love with male vigor because they had not outgrown their adolescent emotions? Or was the interpretation of the theme not to their liking? Their displeasure brought Nijinsky into the newspapers in defense of his art. Many interviews were published, but the *Musical Courier* claimed to have "the only authentic and authorized interview in America on the subject of his art by Vaslav Nijinsky."

"In *Narcisse*, a mythological poem, the role is idealized. The beautiful, slender youth, in love with his own graceful image, is in the dawn of manhood, the first sweet flush of life. What could be more natural than to enter into his spirit, to return to the days of one's youth? This is my role in *Narcisse*. Beautiful dreams of boyhood! There is no virility, only a boyish pureness. That is the way *Narcisse* should be danced. Effeminate it is not! For even in adolescence, a boy is not a girl. True, he is not yet a man, any more than she is a woman, but there the resemblance ends. *His thoughts and desires are different, therefore his movements are different.* [This is a noteworthy statement. It defines the difference between acrobatics and dancing, between tap routines and traditional postures and pirouettes on toe, and the art of expressing life and feeling in the form of ballet.]

"It is for this very reason that one cannot compare with any degree of fairness a male and a female dancer. Their technique and acting may vary—now better, now equal, now worse—but their temperaments remain forever a thing apart. Consequently, there can be no single standard . . . in fact, it is safe to assume that sex has no bearing whatsoever. There is no country in art [here Nijinsky seems to challenge one of the first principles of Fokine], so why be a stickler for 'gender'? After all, what does it matter? But critics, eager for carping or to hide deficiencies in appreciation, seize upon this point."

At the end of the 1916-17 season, Diaghileff's contract was not renewed. It was said that Nijinsky insisted on his absence when he signed a contract with Mr. Kahn. Diaghileff left with sixteen of his dancers including Massine, and Nijinsky was given entire charge as director, ballet master and dancer.

The story of Diaghileff is filled with unhappy personal incidents. A man of remarkable taste and talent, he alienated one after another of the artists he admired and promoted his rage for "novelty." His possessive fury and tragic display of a deepseated sense of social inferiority with its complementary brashness, marred his establishing a permanent Russian Ballet in Europe and America.

CHAPTER VI

NIJINSKY BALLET RUSSE, 1916-17

Pavlowa and Mordkin had been a magnificent dance team. American audiences had seen the finest adagios in the repertoire of the Russian Ballet—adagios created by Petipa, the traditionalist, and by Fokine, the humanist. It had also seen Pavlowa in Fokine's *Seven Daughters of the King of the Black Mountains,* based on the Russian poet Lermontov's poem, *The Three Palms,* the Gertrude Hoffman Ballet Russe in a pirated version of *Schéhérazade,* and Diaghileff's American season of Fokine, Petipa and Nijinsky and Massine choreography. It was likewise familiar with the Oriental Dances of Ruth St. Denis and the "Greek" dancing of Isadora Duncan.

A careful study of the newspaper and magazine reviews of this period indicates that what Americans wanted when they attended a performance of dance, was beauty and grace in woman, virility in man, skillful solo and adagio variations, romantic (preferably German, Austrian or Polish) music, elaborate costumes and spectacular settings. They wanted to enjoy themselves; not to be made aware of their own deeper feelings, not to be stirred in spirit and moved to pity or terror. They did not want their conventions disturbed.

Yet this is precisely what the choreography of Nijinsky did. He created only four ballets:

> *L'Après-Midi d'un Faune,* 1912
> *Jeux,* 1913
> *Le Sacre du Printemps,* 1913
> *Til Eulenspiegel,* 1916

The second was dropped from Diaghileff's repertoire after a few performances; *Sacre* was given only six times; *Til Eulenspiegel* was performed four times in New York and three times in Boston. But the impact of what Nijinsky said and the way in which he said it, has had more influence on his and the suc-

192

ceeding generation of choreographers and dancers than Fokine's sixty-four ballets and all the so-called "modern" dancers of Europe and the United States who, with the exception of the Ballet Jooss, Harald Kreutzberg and Doris Humphrey, were very poor imitations or adulterations of his classic realism.

A summary of Nijinsky's comment on the society of his time is an affirmation of faith in the Catholic pattern. He demonstrated the true character of materialism.

"The twentieth century worships physical strength and physical love, which is not love but lust." Nijinsky's ballets removed the dresses and the draperies that romantic tradition had preserved, and stripped the twentieth century bourgeois, revealing him as a splendid if brutish creature.

The all-important thing about Nijinsky's work was its objectivity. He did not arraign society nor indulge his personal sentiments.

The Story of *Le Sacre du Printemps* is the story of the birth of human emotion in a savage, primitive herd. After appropriate rites and ceremonies, the most beautiful maiden is sacrificed to the Goddess of Spring, symbol of fertility.

The theme of this work is essentially that of the Catholic ritual. The body must be sacrificed to save the soul. But the development given Nijinsky's ballet was classic and realistic although, as a Pole and a Catholic, he could not create a work on this subject without religious overtones.

Its first performance in Paris, on May 29, 1913, in the Theatre des Champs-Elysées, created a near-riot. The fashionable, sophisticated audience was not prepared to be told that the common man in the twentieth century was primitive and savage, and that the worship of physical beauty and male strength could be the undoing of the human race. This was heresy to the followers of Darwin, to the masters of science who had created a religious cult of their own, and to the beneficiaries of the "machine age."

But if Nijinsky did not arraign the constitution of contemporary society, he created a new technique of dance movement, dismissing for his immediate purpose the customary romantic vocabulary of charm and elegance, expressed by the curved line, the pirouette and the "turned-out feet."

Believing that the first and most important thing in the creation of dance was the expression of *an idea* through movement, Nijinsky used movement as a writer uses words, as a musician uses the notes on a scale. He was not content, as Duncan and Fokine had been, to create dances that expressed emotion or dramatic action. In all his work, every movement is penetrated by a living idea.

In Nijinsky's biography by his wife, she described in one paragraph the tremendous field opened to choreographers and dancers by the simple device of giving movement a "literary" sense, by saying that gesture had the same power as the word.

"The 'antique,' the 'medieval,' the 'classic,' and the 'romantic' were different schools to Nijinsky. . . . His conception of the art of dancing was limitless, its variety of modes infinite. He took his first radical step by attacking the idea which was closest to most of us, by rejecting grace, charm, fluency, and the whole classic technique. He created a new technique and demonstrated that the classical steps, such as entre-chats, pirouettes, tours en l'air, could also be made by eliminating the whole school based on the five positions. Any imaginable movement is good in dancing *if it suits the idea which is its subject, but it has to be based on some formulated technique.* . . . For Nijinsky, the conception of art is to express the most one can with as few simple gestures as possible. The nineteenth-century maîtres de ballet entrusted the dramatic part of their ballets to pantomimists who acted without dancing, while the ballerinas danced without acting. They concentrated on the perfection of their vocabulary of steps, regardless of the idea of the drama or period, décor or costume. Nijinsky always rebelled against this grace of form for the mere sake of grace. To express a *literary* and a *moral idea was his aim and therefore he brought acting and dancing together through the medium of movement."*

No other choreographer defined his age so completely as did Nijinsky. He may be said to have interpreted the early twentieth century in dance drama as perfectly as Rabelais interpreted the society of the Middle Ages in prose, and Molière that of absolute monarchy in comedy.

Nijinsky's *Jeux,* a ballet about a game of tennis, is a picture of court life—a court where the young, rich and idle dedicate themselves to "sport" and the mastery of "speed" in their effort to escape boredom and to experience excitement and pleasure.

L'Après Midi d'un Faune is the reverie of Don Juan.

Le Sacre du Printemps is a dance drama about the character and folk ways of the peasant in an age of science and industrial development.

Til Eulenspiegel, programmed as a ballet comi-dramatique, is the story of a town and townspeople plagued by a spirit of independence which must be sacrificed to the cause of order.

Til Eulenspiegel was produced at the Manhattan Opera House in New York on October 24, 1916, with costumes and décor by Robert Edmond Jones, whom Nijinsky described as a greater color artist than Bakst, to music by Richard Strauss.

The evening passed in a tempest of applause. The most "recalcitrant" critics expressed their admiration, and the headlines read: "Nijinsky Wins a Triumph," "An Admirable Performance," "Brilliant and Spectacular," "Nijinsky's Merry Pranks Raise a Riot."

The theme of *Til* was inspired by a German folk story. But the choreography was the creative vision of a poet. The wag, Til Owlglass, who defied the respectable and would champion the poor, who mocked at law and masqueraded in the robes of holiness, the roguish, irrepressible character who symbolized freedom and independence, was in the end put to death by the representatives of the law and order he had defied "while the rabble wept."

American criticism understood this ballet although "it contained little dancing." The symbolism was perfectly clear to audiences in New York and Boston which, because the work required a very large cast and many rehearsals, could not be performed on the road.

A review of the published comments gives first honors to the choreographer, and second to the designer of the set and costumes, who may have been thinking of our own grotesque overhanging towers and dark slums when he said in an interview about his work for Nijinsky:

"I have taken a medieval setting and tried to extract all the grotesqueness and whimsicality possible for stage uses. My poor people appear in the forlornest rags and the scantiest that are possible. My ladies wear the longest trains they can, and still walk, and their headdresses are the tallest a woman can bear without fainting. So it is with the scene. I use the blackness that expresses the medieval, and on it I impose all the fancifulness of design and color that I can muster."

The *New York Herald* reviewed the first performance in the following words:

"A brilliant performance—probably the most brilliant that the Ballet Russe has done in America. . . . Only one choreographic creation of Mr. Nijinsky, *L'Après Midi d'un Faune* has been seen here, and that with another dancer in the principal role. That was the most startling of all of last season's ballets. But in *Til,* Mr. Nijinsky has gone one step further. He has created something entirely new. From the time the curtain went up on a magical, fantastic setting, showing a medieval town, until it was dropped at the close of the ballet, *Til* was fascinating. With the *Faun* and Fokine's *Petrouchka,* it forms a trio of mimic masterpieces. All told, the new production is a triumph of choreography and stage craft and is set to the best modern music obtainable."

Hiram K. Motherwell commented:

"This fluid and human characterization, softened by the dancer's art and heightened by the actor's genius, is not a part of the Nijinsky we have known. One was not prepared for the magnificent verve and vitality of this performance. Analysis might show that this is the same art which Nijinsky has shown of old, cleverly molded to a new end. But it seems more likely that a new part of his genius has found expression. . . . As for the dancers, they have caught Nijinsky's spirit; they had digested his instruction. With liveliness and humor, with perfect control, they went through their unaccustomed parts. They carried out one of the most original and spirited productions the Russian Ballet has yet made."

The skeptical have only to consult the files of newspapers of the day to confirm the estimates quoted above. Scornful music critics, ardent sticklers for "the integrity of music," wrote that it was little short of marvelous how completely the spirit of Strauss' music was "visualized in the spectacle."

That Nijinsky broke new ground in the use of ballet as a commentary on social conditions may be seen by the list of ballets conceived and created in the twenties and thirties by Ballet Jooss, by Leonid Massine, by Serge Lifar, and young American choreographers and dancers.

"As for the theme itself, we may admit that it is a strange and novel one, and that by making use of it Nijinsky seems to be claiming that a fresh range of subject should be opened up, or rather re-opened, for the dance. But this implies, not a destruction of what has been valued in the past and will go on being valuable, but a gradual evolution toward a new expressiveness and a new technique. Strange things are bound to happen. Yet if reason and courage are behind them, why should we be afraid? Prettiness is very well in its way, but life is greater, and truth greater still. And in this truth—this reality which is the gleam that forever eludes us—lies, as some believe, the hope of truest beauty.

"This, at any rate, was the hope of Nijinsky, for, in his own brave words, 'La Grace, le Charme, le Joli sont ranges tout autour du point central qu'est le Beau. C'est pour le Beau que je travaille.' "*

The tour of the Diaghileff Russian Ballet, under the direction of Nijinsky, included in the repertoire many old favorites, little that was new in choreography. But the audiences from the East to the West Coast came to see the greatest stage personality since Caruso's debut.

Overburdened with administrative responsibility, Nijinsky found it difficult to attend the social functions planned in his honor. His recall to serve in the Russian Army made it necessary for him to make a rapid trip to Washington for permission to fulfill the terms of his contract with Otto Kahn. The season of Russian Ballet closed in the spring of 1917 with no permanent home in sight for the artists. Diaghileff was re-assembling a "new" organization with Leonid Massine as successor to Fokine and Nijinsky. English dancers were joining the exiled survivors of the Imperial Ballet Russe on the French Riviera, as well as a new generation of young Russian artists. From 1917 to 1929, two companies produced Russian Ballet in Europe. The Soviet State Ballet carried on, after one dark year, in Russia. The Imperial traditions were respected in France and England by the Ballet Russe de Monte Carlo.

In the United States, while the Denishawns were developing and schooling American dancers in the art of pantomime, the Delsarte system of expression and theatrical dancing, Michel Fokine and Mikhail Mordkin established schools where the classic and romantic ballet principles and techniques were taught with integrity and tireless devotion.

* From Geoffrey Whitworth's *The Art of Nijinsky.*

CHAPTER VII

MICHEL FOKINE

When Morris Gest invited Michel Fokine to create the dances for *Aphrodite,* a spectacular musical play adapted from the novel by Pierre Louys, the famous choreographer was in Scandinavia. On leave of absence from Russia where he worked with the State Ballet, Fokine and his wife had been stranded during a revolution in Finland and were supporting themselves by giving lessons and performances in Sweden, Norway and Denmark, having exhausted the money the Soviet authorities had allowed them to take for travelling expenses.

When he sailed up the bay of New York, the Russian artist is said to have been "enthralled" by the sight of the sky-scrapers, to have exclaimed, "Gorgeous . . . magnificent . . . like nothing I ever saw," and to have looked kindly on the suggestion that he do a ballet on the sky-scrapers.

That was left for an American to do, however. But Fokine, true to his intention to include one work on an American theme in his repertoire, composed *Thunderbird,* a ballet that stemmed, like some of Ted Shawn's, from an Aztec legend.

Thunderbird, produced on the third of September, 1921, at the Hippodrome in New York, in a review called *Get Together,* with music taken from the works of Balakirev, Borodin, Glinka, Rimsky-Korsakoff and Tchaikovsky, and costumes by Willy Pogany, ran for twenty consecutive weeks, the first ten with Michel and Vera Fokine in the principal roles.

The program printed this scenario (adapted from an old Aztec legend by Vera Fokine):

"Returning from a successful hunt, Aztec warriors are performing ritual dances around sacrificial fires. Suddenly, a violent storm breaks, which drives them to take refuge in the temple. Amidst the roaring thunder and flashes of lightning, a flock of 'thunder birds' alight, led by Nahua, a beautiful Toltec princess, who, by the wiles of a wicked magician, has been changed into

198

a bird. From the temple door, Aztlan, the chief of the tribes, perceives the fluttering and enchanted bird and falls in love with Nahua. He attempts to catch her, but she eludes him and flies away with the others. Grieving at her departure, Aztlan calls the Master of Mystic Forces, and asks him to capture the beautiful bird by his magic.

"The Master with his attendants begins to cast the spell, and suddenly there appears growing from the earth a golden tree whose branches entangle Nahua as she comes flying through the air. Aztlan dashes toward the struggling bird, but stops as if turned to stone by her marvelous beauty. Hearing the birds' piercing cries, all the warriors come running and perceive that their chief has been turned into a statue. They take their bows and arrows and shoot at the birds. But at this moment Aztlan comes to his senses and throws himself before his loved one to protect her. The arrows pierce his breast and he falls, mortally wounded. He has sacrificed his life for beauty.

"But the deed of love performs a miracle. The tree begins to blossom with wonderful flowers, and opening its branches, frees Nahua, who is restored as a beautiful girl.

"Approaching Aztlan with tears of sorrow, she performs a healing dance around him. He returns to life. The Master of Mystic Forces unites the lovers, and the whole tribe, overjoyed, greets them with an Aztec war dance."

If the American public had had any doubt about the theatrical fertility of the creator of *Petrouchka* and his versatility, that doubt was short-lived. He was such a master-craftsman that he could not only design a spectacular ballet about the riotous fête of a courtesan (his bacchanale for Aphrodite was posed mainly on an immense staircase), interpret Aztec Indian folklore with poetic charm, and direct ballets for such performers as Gilda Gray and Gertrude Hoffman, but he also produced two ballets for the man who might well be called America's master impresario, Florenz Ziegfeld.

In 1923, Fokine produced two ballets for the Ziegfeld Follies —*Frolicking Gods* and *Farljandio*. The first, to the music of Tchaikovsky's *Casse Noisette Suite,* with scenery by Joseph Urban and costumes by John Reynolds, was a frolicsome story in the *Coppelia* tradition which was honored by the authors and producers of *One Touch of Venus.* As Fokine developed the theme, two lovers, having stayed after closing time, are locked up in a museum. They are dancing in the midnight revels of the Greek statues who come to life when mortals are out of sight, but attendants hear the tumult of merrymaking and break in to find the lovers as naked as the marble statues. The hapless mortals who dared celebrate as gods are taken to the police station and the statues resume their pedestals.

Frederick King commented that the Ziegfeldian climax could hardly have been suggested for a European stage, although *Frolicking Gods* was later performed in England.

Farljandio, with a scenario by John Reynolds and music by Victor Herbert, was a "dance of allurement." The scene is Sicily. The maidens are gypsies.

In 1924, the Fokines organized an "American Ballet," composed of their best students. The company made its debut in association with Michel and Vera Fokine at the Metropolitan Opera House on February 26. Three new works by Fokine were presented: *Elves*, arranged in two parts to music by Mendelssohn, *Overture to the Midsummer Night's Dream* and *Andante* and *Allegro* from the Violin Concerto by Mendelssohn.

The pupils who distinguished themselves particularly were Doris Niles, who became a popular dancer at the Capitol Theatre, and Raymond Guerard, who later changed his first name to Roland and appeared as a soloist in Colonel W. de Basil's Ballet Russe.

Other new works included *Medusa*, a ballet tragedy arranged to Tchaikovsky's *Symphonie Pathetique*, and *Ole Toro*, a ballet of Spanish inspiration to music by Rimsky-Korsakoff.

From 1924 until his death in 1942, Michel Fokine created new ballets for his own company, for producers of musical plays, variety shows, dance teachers, women's clubs, and toward the end of his life, for Ballet Theatre. He toured with his company and appeared at the Hollywood Bowl and at the Lewisohn Stadium.

In 1930, Morris Gest discussed a plan to film the ballets of Fokine, and to organize a school of the ballet. Fokine closed his New York school and went to Hollywood only to be told by the magnates of the film world that his work was too serious and that he was too "artistic."

However, the Ballets Russes of Colonel W. de Basil, with

headquarters in Monte Carlo, were performing *Les Sylphides* and *Petrouchka,* and the Committee of the Academic Ballet of Petrograd had written on the occasion of the twenty-fifth anniversary of Fokine's stage career, in 1923:

"Petrograd is honoring you these days with the sincerest and greatest respect, just as if you were now among your friends and admirers. I take this happy opportunity of expressing to you my deep regret at your long absence, and desire to remind you that for five years your fellow workers have been upholding your artistic succession."

It is impossible to overemphasize the importance of Fokine's principles in the development of theatrical dancing and pantomime. He humanized what had become nothing more than gymnastic exercise and stock gestures, by appealing to the sense of natural beauty, not to the desire for grotesque effects and startling tricks of physical virtuosity.

"Above all," he said, "dancing should be interpretative. It should not degenerate into mere gymnastics. It should in fact be the plastic word. The dance should explain the spirit of the actors in the spectacle. More than that, it should express the whole epoch to which the subject of the ballet belongs. . . . Through the rhythms of the body the ballet can find expression for ideas, sentiments, emotions. The dance bears the same relation to gesture· that poetry bears to prose. Dance is the poetry of motion."

Fokine was true to these principles in all his work. Neither so great an actor nor so great a dancer as Nijinsky, nor possessed of the classic realism of the younger artist, his mastery of the craft of theatrical dancing and of the composition of pantomime has seldom been surpassed. He addresses all classes and races of men; neither revolution nor fashion nor experimental science, nor dogma, concern or oppose him.

CHAPTER VIII

COLONEL W. DE BASIL'S BALLETS RUSSES DE MONTE CARLO

The audience that attended the opening performance of the successor to the Diaghileff Ballets Russes, at the St. James Theatre in New York on December 22, 1933, was not of one mind about the merits of the performance.

Some murmured, "Oh, yes, but then you know I saw Nijinsky in 1916 . . ." Others recalled the Diaghileff Ballet in Paris before the war. Newspaper accounts differed in their judgment of the company made up of young dancers who had studied in the Paris studios of Imperial Russian ballerinas.

The names of the members of Colonel de Basil's Ballets Russes evoked no memories. Toumanova, Baronova, Riabouchinska, Verchinina, Shabelevski, Lichine, Eglevsky, Petroff, Woizikowski—ah, there was a name that stirred a memory. He had been with the original Diaghileff Company . . . but not one of the stars.

Massine was the artistic director. Massine was remembered for his playing of Nijinsky's roles in Diaghileff's American season; he had even stirred the New York police to action over his too literal interpretation of the Faun.

Massine, like Fokine and Mordkin, had left Europe to earn his living in the United States. In 1930, the year after Diaghileff's death, he had become ballet master at the Roxy Theatre. He "worked like a slave over the two-a-day and sometimes more performances." His artistic soul groaned over the demands of a large stage for an over-filled performance of *Scheherazade*. But he stayed with the Roxy for three years, until he became the artistic director of Colonel de Basil's company.

The dancers of Colonel de Basil's Ballets Russes de Monte Carlo did not arrive in New York until a few days before the scheduled opening performance, and the harassed artistic director was up all night "with the lighting system of the St. James

202

Theatre" and because the stage hands were unfamiliar with ballet requirements.

The audience, too, was unfamiliar with the kind of Russian Ballet they saw on December 22, 1933. The program included *Concurrence* (Competition), a satire by Georges Balanchine, with music by Georges Auric, and scenery and costumes by Andre Derain; *Presages* (Destiny), a choreographic symphony by Leonid Massine to the music of Tchaikovsky's *Fifth Symphony*, with scenery and costumes by Andre Masson; and *Le Beau Danube* (The Beautiful Danube), a character ballet by Leonid Massine, with music by Johann Strauss, and costumes and décor after Constantin Guys.

This was more like a French Imperial Ballet! The barbaric splendor that Paris audiences had found in the pre-war performances of the Diaghileff company, the bold splendor of décor by Leon Bakst, the dazzling tonality of Rimsky-Korsakoff, the fierce passion of Borodine, the exuberant sensuality of Moussorgsky were not to be found in the opening night performance of Colonel de Basil's Ballets Russes.

The décor was sophisticated, not bold; the dancing more elegant and spirited than passionate and of elevated character. The libretti and the choreography and the miming appealed more to the mind than to the imagination. This was not vaudeville, nor was it journalism. . . . Ballets Russes de Monte Carlo avoided the awkward exaggeration of social consciousness that hindered German dance and choreography, but it was certainly not poetic.

It was decadent ballet. "There was a turning back not just to simplicity but to simplicities of the past, and to simplicities in different styles which were mingled in pastiche." The de Basil programs showed no sense of style and no creative urge, wrote Ben Ali Haggin. For all the approval of an amiable audience its repertoire was nothing but a "scramble of periods and styles in décor, music and choreography."

On the fifth anniversary of the "resurrection of the Ballet Russe," January 2, 1935, the official souvenir program announced choreographies of sixty-seven ballets by Balanchine, Fokine, Lichine, Massine, Nijinska, Petipa, Romanoff and others.

Composers included were: Adam, Arensky, Auric, Balakirev, Lord Berners, Bizet, Boccherini, Borodine, Brahms, Chabrier, Chopin, Cimarosa, Debussy, Dukelsky, De Falla, Faure, Francaix, Handel, Lambert, Liadoff, Millo, Monte-Clair, Nabakoff, Poulenc, Prokofieff, Rameau, Ravel, Rieti, Rimsky-Korsakoff, Rossini, Satie, Sauguet, Scarlatti, Schumann, Strauss, Stravinsky, Tchaikovsky, Tcherepnine, Weber and others.

Scenery and costumes had been designed "after" or "by": Anisfeld, Annenkoff, Bakst, Bouchene, Comte de Beaumont, Benois, Berard, Braque, de Chirico, Corot, Daboujinsky, Delaunay, Derain, Dufy, Ernest, Gontcharova, Gris, Guys, Johnson, Jokouloff, Korovine, Larionov, Laurencin, Lourie, Masson, Matisse, Miro, Picasso, Pruna, Roerich, Rouot, Scharova, Sert, Tchelicheff, Prine, Schervachidze, Terechkovitch, Utrillo, Zack, and others.

Three hundred and forty or fifty performances were given a year. The company appeared at the Covent Garden Opera House in London, where it gave most of its performances (traditionally, one hundred and eighteen), at the Theatre de Monte Carlo (sixteen performances), at the Grand Theatre de Liceo, Barcelona (twelve performances), and at the Theatre des Champs Elysées, Paris (eighteen performances). The remainder were given in the United States, Mexico, and European countries. Presently, South America was to be included in the tour.

In the United States, the largest part of the program was reserved for the works of Massine, with an occasional revival of an old favorite by Fokine or Petipa, and a Lichine or a Balanchine ballet for variety.

Massine had composed his first ballet, *Soleil de Nuit,* in 1915, at the age of nineteen. Diaghileff, who wanted to train a successor to Nijinsky, had apprenticed "the well-made youth with lustrous brown eyes" to Larionov and Picasso, to learn the principles of the newest movement in art. Massine's next productions were *Las Meninas* (1916), *Les Femmes de Bonne Humeur* (1917), and *Parade* (1917), the first cubist ballet with scenery and costumes by Picasso. This ballet aroused much controversy, but as Massine followed it with a composition entitled *Contes Russes* (1917), a work based on Russian folk dances with scenery and costumes by Larionov and Gontcharova, the influence of the Spanish painter and the revolt against romanticism do not seem to have altered the character of the Moscow-born actor and dancer very profoundly.

Cyril Beaumont lists Massine's principal choreographic works in four parts:

First Diaghileff Period (1915-20)

The four ballets described above, and

Les Jardins d'Aranjuez (1918)

La Boutique Fantasque (1919)

Le Tricorne (1919)

Pulcinella (1920)

Le Chant du Rossignol (1920)

In this group Beaumont also includes Massine's version of *Le Sacré du Printemps.*

Second Diaghileff Period (1924-28)

Les Matelots (1925)

Zephyre et Flore (1925),

Costumes and scenery by Braque

Le Pas d'Acier (1927)

Ode (1928)

De Basil Period (1932-36)

Le Beau Danube (1933)

Scuola di Ballo (1933)

Jeux D'Enfants (1933)

Les Presages (1933)

Choreartium (1933)

Beach (1933)

Union Pacific (1934)

Le Bal (193?)

Jardin Public (1935)

Symphonie Fantastique (1936)

In addition, Massine appeared in and composed ballets for the Ida Rubinstein Company in Paris, the Cochran productions in London, the Roxy in New York, and the Scala Theatre in Milan.

There must also be added the ballets Massine created for Ballet Theatre, the best of which is *Aleko,* and his *Nobilissima Visione* or *St. Francis* set to the *gebraucht musik* of Hindemith, a work produced by the René Blum Monte Carlo Ballets Russes at the Metropolitan Opera House in New York after Monsieur Blum, one-time associate of Colonel de Basil, left that gentleman and organized his own company.

What are the essential characteristics of Massine's ballets? What do they say?

At his best, Massine is the child of Fokine. In his early ballets, *Conte Russes, Tricorne,* and *Boutique Fantasque,* the line of enchantment of *Les Sylphides* and *Petrouchka* is not lost.

The function of the ballet is to tell a story, a fable in movement, mime, dance, within the boundaries of its own world . . . fantasy, satire, drama or comedy. Within this world the Russian Ballet believed in itself . . . and so compelled the public to believe in it. Fairy story? Oh yes, but more truth than what you read in the daily paper.

But when Massine began to yield to the sophisticated appetite of Paris, "when the grave telling of some bright tale that gives the ballet its roots and the dancer her heritage, was ousted by the chic, and the amusing," Caryl Brahms pronounced the integrity of Ballet Russe was lost.

Yet even in his best work, Massine never equalled Fokine. The typical Massine ballet was based on amused observation, not, as in the case of Fokine, on a sensitive understanding of humanity. And for all his pre-occupation with "light and shade," with counterpoint of group against solo dancing, with a balance between dynamic movement and pure plastique, Massine was a tyro at composition by comparison with Fokine.

Massine strangled his theme by a multiplicity of detail. Is the reason for this the fact that Massine was by nature a character actor, and that a classic line was too much for him to achieve?

His ballets are peopled with "characters," or with allegorical symbols and creatures of fantasy. There are no human beings in the tableaux Massine animates, with the single exception of the hero in *Aleko.* Here we have an attempt to create the character of a man. It is an unsuccessful attempt, not because the man Aleko is a failure, but because Massine does not know the reason he fails.

Aleko might be compared with Hamlet—a young aristocrat who is too weak to fight the evils of aristocratic society and yet fancies himself strong enough to live among gypsies.

Massine shows us Aleko as he joins the gypsy camp. We do not know what he ran away from. We do not see his antagonist in the fashionable world he deserts. We must guess from what he flies until the last scene of the ballet, at which time a rich and vain woman is seen holding court while a band of peasants are turned away heartlessly. Had the choreographer begun with a scene in which Aleko, revolted by the selfish cruelty of the vain lady, refuses her attentions and leaves her for a gypsy love, the ballet would have more meaning. As it is, it lacks creative vision.

In his choreographical symphonies, Massine tried to add a choreographic line to a musical work. He did not, as did Isadora Duncan, seek to incarnate the sensuous feeling of music. He constructed a plastic illustration which interpreted the musical text.

Massine's plastic illustrations of Beethoven and Brahms were attempts to create dance dramas but *Presages,* the *Seventh Symphony, Choreartium,* and *Symphonie Fantastique* were symphonic spectacles—nothing more.

When, in 1938-39, Colonel de Basil and René Blum each went his own way, Massine followed the latter. The René Blum Company, sponsored by Universal Art, Inc., with Julius Fleischmann as president and Sergei Denham as vice-president, was managed by S. Hurok. Among the members of the René Blum Company, which took the name of Ballet Russe de Monte Carlo, the following dancers appeared in the 1938-39 season: Massine, Lifar, Alexandra Danilova, Tamara Toumanova, Alicia Markova, Mia Slavenska, Igor Youskevitch, Frederick Franklin, Nathalie Krassovska, Eugenie Delarova, Lubov Roudenko, Marc Platoff and Roland Guerard (American dancers), George Zoritch, Lubov Rostova, Simon Semenoff, and Milada Mladova.

In the de Basil Company, Lichine replaced Massine as premier danseur.

But Colonel de Basil owned the rights to all the Massine ballets as well as those of Fokine, Lichine, Petipa and Nijinsky. He assembled a company with an American prima ballerina, Texasborn Nana Gollner and, with permanent headquarters in Buenos Aires, which fared well, although Nana Gollner returned to the United States to join Ballet Theatre.

Ballet Russe de Monte Carlo, with Massine as artistic director (1938-42), produced not only the traditional Fokine, Nijinsky, Petipa and Massine works, but a few Balanchine and Nijinska ballets and several ballets on American themes: *The New Yorker,* by Massine, with music by George Gershwin and décor by Rea Irwin; *Saratoga,* by Massine, with music by Jaromir Weinberger and décor by Oliver Smith; *Ghost Town,* by Marc Platoff, with music by Richard Rodgers and décor by Raoul Pene du Bois, and libretto by Platoff and Rodgers; and in 1942-43, under the direction of David Libidins, *Rodeo* or *The Courting at Burnt Ranch*, by Agnes de Mille, with music by Aaron Copland, scenery by Oliver Smith, and costumes by Kermit Love.

It is interesting to see how Massine treated the subject of the United States in the medium of ballet. He composed three "American" ballets: *Union Pacific*, to a libretto by the American poet Archibald McLeish, as well as the above-mentioned *Saratoga* and *The New Yorkers*. None of these compositions show any understanding of the nature and character of the American nation. At best, they mirror the man-around-town's grasp of the history of a strong, violent, often selfish, usually kind people.

Mr. Massine's collaborators had one foot in Paris and the other in the cities of our eastern seaboard. It was impossible for him not to be trapped into accepting, on its face value, a bogus sophistication this country knew nothing at all about. The building of the first transcontinental railroad was a subject much more suited to Borodine and Fokine than to Nabokoff, McLeish and Massine.

Horse Racing at Saratoga, with décor by Renoir and music by Victor Herbert or Rudolph Friml, might perhaps have been a second *Le Beau Danube. The New Yorker* should not have been done at all; or, if so, it should have been entitled *Café Society*.

The American works by American choreographers are discussed in other chapters. That our choreographers are indebted to Russian leadership, teaching and inspiration, must be and is here acknowledged with sincere appreciation.

CHAPTER IX

LINCOLN KIRSTEIN'S "AMERICAN BALLET"

THE COUNTER-REVOLUTION OF 1934-36

In an impressive and important book entitled *The Birth of Ballets Russes*, Prince Peter Lieven discusses the post-war ballet with such clarity that it seems urgent to quote from his analysis.

After writing that, firstly, a new ballet art had been created, in that the old classical Imperial Ballet was revolutionized by replacing fantasies in the old traditional rut with productions of a vital dramatic content, Prince Peter Lieven emphasizes the fact that this revolution was accomplished in the first years of Ballets Russes (1909-11) . . . in the Fokine ballets, *Les Sylphides, Prince Igor, Schéhérazade, Carnaval,* and *Petrouchka.*

Then in 1912, before the public had had time to assimilate the Fokine revolution, came the second revolution in choreography—the Nijinsky revolution, distinguished "by a complete break with classicism and by a striving for novelty." Prince Lieven calls this form of ballet "the modernism which is to dominate in the post-war period."

Was this a rage for trifles to distract the conscience from accepting the consequences of the war and its significance? The Russian author does not believe very heartily in "Modernism."

"In my opinion, the basic convention of ballet is the classic dance with its five positions, points, entrechats, pirouettes, and so on. This is the choreographic scale. It is equally limitless in its possible developments. Allied with character-dances and mimes, it offers a free field for the choreographer.

"To create a new choreographic basis, a new school of ballet independent of the classic, is no easy matter. To do this, takes decades, if not centuries. The chaotic jumble of 'free' movements must be crystallized into a new 'scale' of its own in order to create a new tradition, a new convention. Isolated cases may be successful, but on this style ballet can not be constructed. Isadora

209

Duncan was a miracle, but what is more of a nightmare than those ladies who, following her example, danced on bare feet round the world?

"In the United States, post-war ballet was either 'Russian' or 'modern.' The Russian companies produced pre-war Diaghileff. 'Modern dance' was the concern of American dancers. Then in 1933, the word went around that two young men were launching an 'American School of Ballet,' that at last America was to have her own ballet company and that 'from all the dancing schools of the forty-eight states, would be culled the ballerinas.' "

Lincoln Kirstein and Edward Warburg had decided that American themes could be interpreted by the entrechat, the pirouette, the glissade and the tour jeté.

George Balanchine was invited to head the school and to form the company. The brilliant young Russian choreographer, not yet twenty-five, had created the following ballets for Diaghileff:

		Music	Décor
1925	The Nightingale	Stravinsky	Matisse
1925	Barabau	Rieti	Utrillo
1927	Pastorale	Auric	Pruna
1927	Triumph of Neptune	Berners	Pollock
1927	Jack-in-the-Box	Satie	Derain
1927	The Cat	Sauguet	Gabo-Pevsner
1928	The Gods Go A-Begging	Handel	Bakst: Juan Gris
1928	Apollon	Stravinsky	Bauchant
1929	The Ball	Rieti	Chirico
1929	Prodigal Son	Prokofieff	Rouault

After Diaghileff's death in Venice in 1929, Balanchine created three new ballets for the de Basil Ballets Russes de Monte Carlo.

Cotillon	Chabrier	Bérard
Bourgeois Gentilhomme	Strauss	Benois
Concurrence	Auric	Derain

In 1933, Balanchine founded "Les Ballets, 1933." He created six new ballets which were presented in Paris with applause from the hothouse intellectuals, and in London to an embarrassing silence. These ballets, for which "advance guard" poets supplied libretto material, were:

Mozartiana	Mozart	Berard
L'Errante	Schubert	Tchelitchev
Les Songes	Milhaud	Derain
Fastes	Sauguet	Derain
Seven Capital Sins	Kurt Weil	Neher
The Waltzes	Beethoven	Terry

Balanchine accepted Kirstein and Warburg's offer. In October, 1933, he arrived in New York to found a school "rooted in the traditions of the classic ballet," and to develop a permanent ballet company whose members would be a product of the school.

The Story of the American Ballet, by Ruth Eleanor Howard, contains the following description of the principles and purposes of Kirstein, Warburg and Balanchine.

"At first, by the very nature of its beginning, the company would be part of the school, but the ultimate aim was that the two would be separate; the school training pupils for and graduating them into the company, and the company not only sustaining itself, but providing support for the school so that it could continue its work of developing dancers. Obviously, however, at the outset, the ballet company was composed entirely of students in the school. A further hope incorporated in the original idea was for an annual tour of the country, thus building up a nation-wide ballet audience."

But these fine hopes did not altogether materialize. A ballet company that gives performances after one year of training was not a professional group ready to compete with such seasoned veterans as "Ballets Russes" or the attractions sponsored by great American impresarios like Florenz Ziegfeld, John Murray Anderson, and Sol Hurok. It soon became apparent that Lincoln Kirstein and his associates had bitten off more than they could chew.

The opening repertoire of the American Ballet Company contained only one work of native inspiration, *Alma Mater,* a cartoon in dance about fauns at play in America's oldest universities.

Unfortunately, the choreography, the music and the décor did not live up to Nijinsky. The story by Edward Warburg, the music by Kay Swift, the décor by John Held were amusing . . . but it was all too superficial to deserve serious attention. *Alma Mater* was little more than a "collegiate" lampoon. The other ballets in the repertoire, *Dreams, Reminiscence, Serenade, Transcendance* and *L'Errante,* were either decadent or trifling divertissements.

Transcendance, by Lincoln Kirstein, was a fantasy. The program announced it a surrealist treatment of a complex theme. "The sleight of hand between night and day, living and dying." At the tryout performance in Hartford, Conn., in December, 1934, a critic wrote:

"In watching the superb elegance of the choreography, the moving dramatic succession of moods from frustration, through the unreal realms of mesmerism back to the ring of earth under merrymakers' heels of peasant dancers, it is all so very tender, so very thrilling, so deeply appealing just from its visual content, so filled with exquisite figures, patterns and rhythms that 'what it means' seems rather unimportant indeed!"

This review acclaimed *Transcendance* as the outstanding feature of the Hartford première. But the New York reviews of the March, 1935, performances at the Adelphi Theatre were chilly. Obviously, no dramatic critics bestirred themselves as they did for Charles Weidman, remarked Frederick King. The outer fringe of music writers were either lukewarm or satirical. Mr. Chotzinoff liked *Reminiscence* because, he said, he didn't have to understand anything. He dismissed *L'Errante* in terms of polite ridicule.

John Martin complained that in the engagement of Mr. Balanchine "once again American artists had been passed by for a high artistic post of which at least half a dozen are eminently fitted." But Mr. Martin did not indicate who these were.

Other critics credited Balanchine with ability in both pantomime and the classic dance, but did not bother to comment on his themes. Many challenged the title of the new organization. Should not an American Ballet give something American? But no critic defined American Ballet. "Large numbers think they can dance an American dance, but surely it is more than three-fourths German." Frederick King wrote this, concluding dryly that some people seemed to think an American dance would come out of the air; should we set about creating a system of choreographic taps?

No one mentioned the fact that six works in the repertoire of the American Ballet were the ballets Balanchine had created for "Ballets 1933." There had not been time to launch a school, rehearse a new company and compose new ballets! As for American librettists and choreographers . . . it was too early for their talents to have ripened.

The American Ballet Company played two weeks in New York, a few times at summer stadium concerts and then, after an ill-fated attempt to tour under the Musical Art Management Corporation, this semi-amateur theatrical troupe concluded its brief life.

However, the ability of the dancers was rewarded, as well as the choreographic technique of Georges Balanchine and the high standard of teaching at the school, when Edward Johnson of the Metropolitan Opera House engaged Balanchine and a group from the American Ballet School to produce and perform the opera ballets at "the Met."

When Edward Johnson announced he had signed a contract for young Americans to do the opera ballets at the first opera house in the world, many eyebrows were lifted. The Metropolitan Opera House might be compared to the Imperial Theatre in Russia. The boxholders who underwrote the deficits and dictated the policy of the historic music hall, knew little or nothing of artists named Lew Christensen, William Dollar, Eugene Loring, Charles Laskey, Annabelle Lyon, Ruthanna Boris, Giselle Caccialanza, Annia Breyman, Holly Howard, Elise Reiman. But Mr. Johnson insisted that the Metropolitan should present not alone excellent dancers but young people endowed with beauty of form and face. The old ballet organization needed new blood and new talent.

Throughout the season, the press was cautious in its comments about the new ballet. The choreography designed by Balanchine offended many an "old subscriber," who lamented the new ballet master's endeavor to reconstruct the style of dances current at the time *Carmen, Gioconda, Tannhäuser* and Aida were placed.

It was said that the ballet interlude in *Carmen* was carried out by Lew Christensen and Rosa Ponselle with more vigor than Spanish feeling, and no great satisfaction was expressed over the *Tannhäuser* ballet in the Bayreuth tradition. Mr. Balanchine was accused of staging an orgy. His private comment was that the scene was in Hell and that in Hell they don't dance a minuet.

The ballet came off better in its assignments for the Sunday night concerts, or to fill out time after a short operatic work. Revivals of the Balanchine repertoire were offered and divertissements in which Lew Christensen, William Dollar and Holly Howard gave excellent performances, notably in the balletic version of Glück's *Orfeo*.

But while the technical mastery of Balanchine as a choreographer was being established for all to recognize, and the American School of the Ballet grew and prospered, and young American dancers won applause for their pirouettes and grandes jetés, what was happening to the young man who had founded the American Ballet? What of Lincoln Kirstein?

When the company attached to the School of American Ballet disbanded in 1936, no American themes were being used by the companies using classic technique and pantomime other than the European Americana of Massine and Michel Fokine's *Thunderbird*. Balanchine had composed a ballet for the musical comedy *On Your Toes* called *Slaughter on Tenth Avenue,* but this brilliant satire might as well have been set in London as in New York. No one was saying anything about America in the medium of classic ballet.

Then Mr. Kirstein conceived the idea of a troupe of dancers who would perform works of native character during the summer season in and about New England. He selected twelve members of the American Ballet, named them "Ballet Caravan," and set about creating a repertoire.

"Caravan" ballets, 1936, 1937, 1938, included:

	Book	*Music*	*Choreography*	*Costumes and Décor*
Pocahontas	Kirstein	E. Carter, Jr.	Lew Christensen	Free
Filling Station	Kirstein	Virgil Thomson	Lew Christensen	Cadmus

	Book	Music	Choreography	Costumes and Décor
Yankee Clipper	Kirstein	Paul Bowles	Loring	Charles Rain
Billy the Kid	Kirstein	Aaron Copland	Loring	Jared French
City Portrait	Kirstein	Henry Brant	Loring	
Harlequin for President	Kirstein	Scarlatti	Loring	Keith Martin

Ballet Caravan supplied one great American ballet, *Billy the Kid,* and material in the form of scenarios by Lincoln Kirstein that no other poet of American birth and training had conceived of in dramatic terms. The notable poets, Thomas Stearns Eliot and Archibald McLeish, who left their native Missouri and Illinois for London and Paris, created *The Waste Land* (which might be called *Lament for the Death of Europe*) and a fancy piece of poesy entitled *Conquistador* (which might be called *A Salute to the Spanish Cavalier*). Messrs. Eliot and McLeish were earnest expatriates.

What America was about, is more truthfully told by the Caravan ballets, unpretentious and undeveloped as they were.

A rapid analysis of their themes informs the curious that the American desperado is a dandy and a disappointed cavalier; that American Woman wants to be a lady at any cost; that the American intellectuals were currently dreamers, not thinkers; that "the big city" was a concentration camp; that an age of science had converted the university into an athletic field, and made scholars into satyrs, and that American girls wear their brothers' boots.

Ballet Caravan did not have a long life as an independent organization. Perhaps the very qualities to which it owed its success, prevented its permanent stabilization. Poetry seldom flourishes side by side with routine.

But the influence of its productions inspired the work of Agnes de Mille and a score of young American choreographers and dancers.

Ballet Caravan failed in choreography with the exception of Loring's *Billy the Kid* and Christensen's *Jinx*; folk dance and regional mime provided vaudeville entertainment, not ballet.

It was possibly too much to expect of such young artists. In 1941-42, Mr. Christensen and Mr. Loring had their own company, Dance Players. At this time, Mr. Christensen produced his best ballet, *Jinx*, a story of circus life to the music of Benjamin Britten, with décor by George Bockman. *Jinx* almost achieved the quality of an American *Petrouchka*, with Mr. Christensen in the title role. Mr. Loring's *Prairie*, to the music of Norman Dello Joio, inspired by the poem of Carl Sandburg, was a beautiful dance composition, but too slight in method for its matter. Dance Players had the merit of bringing together a first-rate group of young Americans who continued the Caravan tradition and were later absorbed into larger companies to the mutual benefit of all concerned. Outstanding in the Dance Players, besides Eugene Loring and Lew Christensen, were Janet Reed, Joan McCracken, Freda Flier, Bobbie Howell, Bettina Dearborn, Mary Heater, Michael Kidd, Zachary Zolov, Conrad Linden and Florence Weber, who played the indispensable piano accompaniments with warmth and vigor.

CHAPTER X

THE MORDKIN BALLET

TRIUMPH OF TITANIC MANHOOD—PREMATURE BIRTH OF THE AMERICAN BALLERINA

Mordkin, like Fokine, was honored by the Soviet State as he had been by the Court of Imperial Russia. In 1912, after his second coast-to-coast American tour with the company he had organized after leaving Pavlowa, he returned to Moscow, picked out Alexandra Balashova from the corps de ballet, elevated her to the role of ballerina, and danced with her in a tour of Russia, appearing at the Imperial Theatres of Moscow and Petrograd. In 1914, Mordkin and Balashova danced at the Empire Theatre in London with so much success that they were booked for twelve consecutive weeks.

During the first World War, he collaborated with the Kamerny Theatre of Moscow. His work at the Kamerny Theatre was so outstanding that Constantin Stanislavsky invited him to establish a school of plastique and rhythmics applicable to the spoken drama, in connection with the Moscow Art Theatre.

Although the Government requisitioned Mordkin's school in 1922, he was asked to accept the post of Director of Ballet at the State Academy Theatre. He did so, but his independent spirit soon asserted itself and he preferred to return to the stage. With a new partner, Victorina Krieger, one of the best dancers of the younger generation in Russia, he gave a series of performances in Moscow and toured as far as Siberia; in the mid-1920's he came to New York, participated in several revues, and finally opened a ballet school with classes in New York and Philadelphia.

The Mordkin School did not resemble, either in theory or method, schools directed by followers of Diaghileff. Admirers of Mordkin asserted that no matter how great the achievements of Diaghileff, his remarkable theatre "had carried on to its very end the sin of its builder. Diaghileff was not able to restore the

217

severed harmony between the masculine and the feminine in the ballet." This quotation from Kamischnikoff is part of a brief article which says further with much pith and pertinence that Mordkin was the very antithesis of the semi-masculine ballet dancer, the hyacinthine youth with the delicate features of a girl; that, serving as an example himself, Mordkin had showed how great an artist a man could be in the act of living as a man, not as part of a graceful design.

When the Mordkin Ballet Company, organized in 1936 as an outlet for the advanced students, opened at the Majestic Theatre in New York in 1937, the foreword to the souvenir read:

"The Curtain

"This curtain rises on another chapter of the great career of Mikhail Mordkin.

"He has done today with American boys and girls what was only considered possible with Russian Imperial Ballet a decade ago.

"May his ballet live on indefinitely as an American institution and presented by his disciples in all corners of the world."

This brave hope was realized only indirectly. Great as he was, Mikhail Mordkin could not transform the practical and commercial traditions that had frozen the feelings and spirit of American boys and girls in the brief span of ten years. The youth of a mechanically gifted people found it easier to master the technique required by Balanchine choreography than to master the human understanding of life required by Mordkin's ballets. The latter is based on evaluating the differences among instinct, feeling and mind, without which the dancer achieves no communication of spirit . . . nothing but a pleasing picture or an ingeniously contrived maneuver, those dangerously academic embellishments to the art of the dance, the drama, pantomime or theatre.

The repertoire of the Mordkin Ballet in 1937-38 included as its principal productions *Giselle* (the first performance since 1911, when Mikhail Mordkin as ballet master of the Imperial Russian Ballet made ballet history with Anna Pavlowa as his dancing partner) and *The Goldfish* (in its first performance ever offered to the public), story by Alexander Pushkin, music by Tcherepnine, scenery by Soudeikine.

The principals assisting Mr. Mordkin were:

Chief prima ballerina, Lucia Chase. Miss Chase played the roles of Giselle and of the Fisherman's wife in *The Goldfish*. She made her professional debut in the first American performance of Tchaikovsky's *The Sleeping Beauty*, which the Mordkin Ballet presented in her home town of Waterbury.

First male solo dancer, assistant to Mikhail Mordkin, Leon Varkas, born in Lincoln, Nebraska, educated in Russia in the art of ballet, a premier in the Worker's Ballet performances in Moscow. Leon Varkas played the role of Duke Albrecht opposite Lucia Chase in *Giselle*, and replaced Mordkin in the role of the Fisherman in *The Goldfish* when the company went on tour.

Ballerina, Viola Essen, "without doubt, the youngest ballerina in the world, not yet having celebrated her fourteenth birthday." Born in St. Louis of Bulgarian parents, Viola Essen won scholarships for proficiency in dramatics, piano playing, physical excellence and scholastic accomplishment. She played the fairy goldfish in the Pushkin ballet, and the role of the Queen of the Willis in *Giselle*.

Romantic and comedy dancer, Dimitri Romanoff, a young Russian, former star of the San Francisco Opera Ballet and premier classical dancer in the Pavlev-Oukrainsky Ballet, played Hans in *Giselle*, Chout in *The Goldfish*.

The student company had expected to give one performance at the Majestic Theatre on April 4, 1937, but popular approval held them over three nights before they left for a somewhat extended tour.

The audience was enchanted and the critics had good things to say about the Pushkin ballet to the music of Tcherepnine and the choreography of Mordkin; about Viola Essen's "excellent line" which would better with development (Miss Essen was a candidate for high honors in the classic roles). "Her figure was what Adeline Genée once said was the best possible for a budding ballerina"; the miming of the character dancers was admirable; the role of "Giselle" required an experienced classical ballerina.

In its second season, 1938-39, the Mordkin Ballet presented

Giselle, The Goldfish, La Fille Mal Gardée (for the first time on this continent), *Dionysus,* new creation by Mordkin based on Greek mythology, set to the music of Glazounov, *Swan Lake,* a new symphonic version by Mordkin, with new décor by Lee Simonson, *Voices of Spring,* by Mordkin, with music by Johann Strauss and décor by Lee Simonson, and *Trepak,* a ballet created by Mordkin based on the oldest dance of the Russian people. The music for *Trepak* was by Tcherepnine as dictated to Serge Strenkovsky, the décor was by Soudeikine, and the choreography by Mordkin. The ballet had its world première in the United States.

And in its second year, the Mordkin Ballet added to its principal dancers, promoted some, reclassified others. One of the most important changes was to replace Lucia Chase as prima ballerina; Mikhail Mordkin engaged Patricia Bowman, who for four years had been the leading dancer of the Roxy Theatre and Radio City, two years of which she was the partner of Leonid Massine.

Born in Washington, D.C., Patricia Bowman attended ballet school as a child, and later became the favorite pupil of Michel Fokine. She was one of the only three that Fokine personally taught and authorized to dance *The Death of the Swan,* the other two being Vera Fokina and Anna Pavlowa. Miss Bowman worked daily with Mr. Mordkin for eight months before appearing in any of her new ballet roles. The respect Miss Bowman and Mr. Mordkin indicated for their ballet art in this painstaking preparation, resulted in a complete mastery of such parts as Giselle (the great emotional test of every ballerina), the leading role in *Voices of Spring, The Goldfish,* and *Swan Lake.*

Lucia Chase, with the title of "ballerina," was assigned the role of Lizette in *La Fille Mal Gardée,* and the Bacchanale in *Dionysus.*

Nina Stroganova, ballerina, joined the Mordkin Company, leaving the Ballet Russe of the Paris Opera Comique, where she was prima ballerina.

Karen Conrad, Philadelphia born, and trained under Catherine Littlefield, was promoted, after one year with Mordkin, to first soloist.

Four male dancers were engaged as soloists to assist Leon Varkas, premier danseur.

Edward Caton, born in Russia, of American parentage, trained in the art of ballet in Russia, member of the last Pavlowa company, before joining the Mordkin Ballet was premier danseur for five years at the Chicago Civic Opera Company.

Vladimir Dokoudovsky, great-nephew and pupil of Olga Preobrajenska, was one of the greatest Petrograd ballet dancers and teacher of most of the stars of Europe.

Kari Karnakoski, a native of Helsingfors, Finland, was also a pupil of Mme. Preobrajenska, and a former member of the Monte Carlo Ballet.

Savva Andreieff, son of the famous author of *He Who Gets Slapped,* was formerly a member of Colonel de Basil's Company and René Blum's Ballet Russe de Monte Carlo.

The repertoire and the male dancing were applauded, but the American ballerinas, for all their good will and hard work, were neither emotionally nor technically ready for the roles they attempted to interpret. The cold brilliance of Karen Conrad excepted, the group of feminine dancers suggested either vaudeville specialty numbers, musical comedy, or soubrette roles in operettas. None of them even occasionally displayed the inner strength of character and spirit necessary to achieve the dramatic authority and elegance of true ballerinas.

CHAPTER XI

BALLET THEATRE—ANTON DOLIN AND ANTONY TUDOR

In the fall of 1939, the Mordkin Ballet was reorganized. It was presented by Advanced Arts Ballets, Inc., under the name of the Ballet Theatre and staged by what was described in the official program as "the greatest collaboration in ballet history."

This naive fanfare was by way of challenging the Diaghileff and Russian Ballets, for Ballet Theatre wanted it known that it intended to "compete in the major league." The foreword to its 1941 season sums up the accomplishments of the first year in such words as "fantastic," "not seriously credible," "staggering," and "astounding." It was solemnly asserted that never once, during the four months of rehearsing and preparing that stretched between the initial announcement and the opening performance at the Centre Theatre in New York, January 2, 1940, had Ballet Theatre backed down on its expressed intention.

But four months of the firmest intention do not guarantee the execution of an over-ambitious program. Ballet Theatre demonstrated, as did so many of its predecessors, that American faith in reckless speed, volume and exaggeration, is a costly and vain gesture.

The Mordkin Ballet and Ballet Russe had one, two, or three choreographers. Ballet Theatre announced eleven: Adolph Bolm, Agnes De Mille, Anton Dolin, José Fernandez, Michel Fokine, Andrée Howard, Eugene Loring, Mikhail Mordkin, Bronislava Nijinska, Yurek Shabelevski, and Antony Tudor.

Twenty principal dancers and twelve soloists headed a company of fifty-six, to which were added a Spanish unit of nineteen and a Negro unit of fourteen.

Eleven designers worked for Ballet Theatre. The ballets in its repertoire were set to the music of eighteen composers. It engaged the services of three conductors.

Of the choreographers, three were Russian: Fokine, Mordkin and Bolm. Two were Poles: Nijinska and Shabelevski. Three were English: Dolin, Howard and Tudor. Two were American: Loring and De Mille.

Four of the eighteen composers: Tchaikovsky, Tcherepnine, Prokofieff and Mossolov, were Russians. Five: Chausson, Debussy, Milhaud, Adam and Honegger, were French. There were four Germans: Schubert, Schumann, Mahler and Kurt Weil; one Spanish composer: Granados; one Austrian: Johann Strauss; and two Americans: Henry Brant and Raymond Scott.

The principal ballets produced at the Centre Theatre included:

La Fille Mal Gardée, restaged by Nijinska.
Giselle, restaged by Anton Dolin.
Swan Lake, restaged by Anton Dolin.
Les Sylphides, revived under the personal direction of Michel
  Fokine.
Carnaval, revived under the personal direction of Fokine.
Mechanical Ballet, by Adolph Bolm.
Jardin aux Lilas, by Antony Tudor.
Dark Elegies, by Antony Tudor.
Judgment of Paris, by Antony Tudor.
Death and the Maiden, by Andrée Howard.
Lady into Fox, by Andrée Howard.
Voices of Spring, by Mikhail Mordkin.
Ode to Glory, by Yurek Shabelevski.
The Great American Goof, by William Saroyan and Eugene
  Loring.
Peter and the Wolf, by Prokofieff and Bolm.
Goyescas, by Alder Jenkins and José Fernandez.
Obeah (Black Ritual), by Agnes de Mille.

In retrospect, the honors for the finest ballet of the season went to Michel Fokine for the superb production of his masterpiece, *Les Sylphides.* The corps de ballet did live up to the advance notices and promises, and the soloists, particularly Karen Conrad, Katharine Sergava, Nina Stroganova and Nana Gollner, deserved the title of ballerina in every sense of the word.

The revivals of *La Fille Mal Gardée, Carnaval,* and *Voices of Spring* were pleasing light entertainment and were so received. The American public did *not* like *Lady into Fox, Death and the Maiden, Goyescas, Mechanical Ballet, Obeah,* and *The Great American Goof.*

Without Anton Dolin and Antony Tudor, the greatest collaboration in the history of ballet would have been a one-man show—Fokine.

Not that the two English artists are to be compared with the great Russian choreographer. Theirs is a special and fine contribution to the art of ballet. It is the creation of a kind of ballet that is not Russian, neither in flavor nor in style; that is not Diaghileff ballet, nor Nijinsky ballet, nor Paris nineteenth or twentieth century ballet. Anton Dolin and Antony Tudor, with the dancers in Ballet Theatre, created a kind of English ballet that Americans would buy tickets to see.

Jean Georges Noverre (1727-1810), French dancer and ballet master who worked with David Garrick in London (1755-57) and was ballet master at the French Opera from 1775 to 1780 and who is considered today as the one who introduced dramatic action into the ballet, wrote in his famous *Lettres sur la Danse et les Ballets,* a work published in 1760, that there are three and only three styles of dancers:

I. The "Danseur Noble," of serious or heroic style.
II. The "Demi-caractère" dancer, of great technique as opposed to pure form.
III. "Danseur Grotesque," or character dancer, who is physically unsuited to lyric or heroic roles.

The success of Anton Dolin's revivals of *Giselle* and *Swan Lake* was undoubtedly due to the fact that Mr. Dolin not only respected the principles of Noverre in casting and directing the ballets he restaged, but that he possessed in his person the physical elegance, fine features and bearing that American audiences wanted to see in the interpreter of the roles of Count Albrecht and Prince Siegfried. The ballerina in *Giselle,* as produced by Ballet Theatre in 1940-41, whether Nana Gollner or Annabelle Lyon, was not as important as the male dancer, Anton Dolin.

He organized the Markova-Dolin group which toured the United States, Central America and Mexico in 1945 to 1948. A year later, he formed a group, with Markova, in England which became London's Festival Ballet, and was artistic director and principal dancer until 1961. Anatole Chujoy described him as "the first English male dancer to earn international fame."

Antony Tudor, as a dancer, belongs to the third category

listed above. But it was not primarily as a dancer that Mr. Tudor made his mark. It was rather as a satirist, as a melancholy commentator on the Victorian manners and morals that rule American country club society, that the Englishman who looks like an Elizabethan lord and lampoons the domestic male and his womenfolk, commanded the new choreography in Ballet Theatre.

Jardin aux Lilas, later re-named *Lilac Garden,* was the most popular "new" ballet of the 1940 season.

More kin to ballroom dancing and pantomime than formal ballet, *Jardin aux Lilas* might be described as the stifled scream of human beings asphyxiated by Correct Convention.

Mr. Tudor, in the role of the husband who symbolized Social Order, gave the most remarkable performance of a character who, thanks to *Life With Father,* has become a household word in the United States.

No review of Ballet Theatre 1940-41 is complete without a comment about its most important failure—a failure which was in its way as important as the success of Fokine, Dolin and Tudor. For when America said "no" to *The Great American Goof,* by Saroyan and Eugene Loring, American audiences were refusing to accept an adolescent attitude as genuine American art.

The full title of *The Great American Goof* was printed in the program as: *A Number of Absurd and Poetic Events in the Life of the Great American Goof.*

William Saroyan listed his characters as follows:

The Great American Goof, the naive white hope of the human race.
The Woman, the bright potential.
The Dummy, tradition and the ordinary.
Policeman, orderly idiocy.
Old Man in Prison, ignorance, age and naiveté.
A little Girl, wisdom not yet educated and spoiled.
Women, sex.
Workers, misfits.
A Student of Karl Marx, an opium addict.
Priest, capitalism.
Drunkard, a religious man, etc.

Mr. Saroyan's own description of the theme of his ballet-play reads:

"As I see it, the living probably deserve nothing better than what they get, one at a time, although this irritates me personally. It irritates me because nobody other than myself seems to understand that the world is not real. That in reality, there is no such thing . . . the world which everyone other than myself seems to have identified and accepted as the world, is in reality a figment in a nightmare of an idiot. No one could possibly create anything more surrealistic and unbelievable than the world which everyone believes is real and is trying very hard to inhabit.

"Willy-nilly, the story of this ballet is on this theme:

"If the world is uninhabitable . . . if it is no fit place for a man of honor and dignity . . . what place should the living inhabit?"

On this theme is written the story of *The Great American Goof.* It is a story of failure—the failure of a young man to find anything worth while in life; a tale of peevish discontent and dilettantism; of the green and callow American snob who imitates the decadent sophisticates of Europe, as the high school dude imitates the slick university rake.

The protagonist in Saroyan's ballet, confronted with a series of difficulties, promptly runs away with the querulous assertion that he wants to resign.

The work concludes with the flight of the hero, but not without a final brandish of the arm! The white hope of the human race addresses a swaggering bit of bombast to his adversaries, "It may take six or seven thousand years, but I'll change the world."

As the author of *My Heart's in the Highlands* and *The Time of Your Life,* a much better piece of work than this was expected of William Saroyan. Why had such a brilliant and talented young writer not said in his ballet libretto, that American workers, far from being misfits, were among the best in the world, but that mechanical skill no longer satisfied them, and that their social consciousness forecast the rise of a new and powerful ruling class deserving of respect and attention?

Why did a promising American poet present Woman as being in one of two categories: "a bright potential" (beautiful and unkind) or "sex"? Woman in America in 1940 was still primarily a domestic convenience entitled "Ma" or "Mrs."

Mr. Saroyan clearly believed the world no fit place for men of honor and dignity . . . but he expected the American public to believe that his hero, the white hope of the human race, would be able to make a new world. Was this fantasy or an unadmitted desire to be part of a "ruling class"?

Saroyan's hero, as presented on the stage in the ballet-pantomime by Eugene Loring, looked like a boy from the country. He moved with agility and with a faun-like quality, not in the least like a callow or clumsy rustic. Eugene Loring's interpretation of the 1940 American hero was far closer to the truth than the author's.

The pantomime in *Goof* was better than the dance designs. Mr. Loring was a character actor. He made the *Goof* an oddly moving creature, and his creation of Dummy, superbly acted by Antony Tudor, almost saved a bad scenario.

The failure of *Goof* was not the fault of its choreographer, actors, dancers, composer, or costume and scenic designer. It was the fault of its poet.

After a short season in Chicago at the Civic Opera, and a few disappointing weeks at the Majestic Theatre in New York where the bright record of the Centre Theatre première was not repeated, Ballet Theatre changed management. In 1942, it became one of the Hurok attractions.

Mikhail Mordkin went back to teaching. Richard Pleasant, who had succeeded him and given Ballet Theatre its name, joined the United States armed forces. Eugene Loring left to act in a play by William Saroyan. *The Great American Goof* was dropped from the repertoire.

Fokine and Tudor were commissioned to create new ballets. Massine was added to the list of choreographers, and the American ballerinas were supplanted by Irina Baranova, justly famed for her classic technique and "demi-caractère" dancing in the role of Lisette in *La Fille Mal Gardée,* and Alicia Markova, at the time the greatest lyric ballerina since Pavlowa.

At the end of the 1942-43 season, which included a coast-to-coast tour, Russian and English choreographers and Alicia Markova had won a new audience for ballet in America. Fokine's *Bluebeard,* a pantomime version of the opera-bouffe by Meilhac and Halevy, to the music of Jacques Offenbach, was gay nonsense that revived a movie-surfeited public. *Princess Aurora,* staged by Anton Dolin after Petipa's choreography with costumes after Bakst, presented a dance spectacle of classic authority in which the younger dancers could be enjoyed as well as the prima ballerinas who alternated in the leading role.

Anthony Tudor's *Pillar of Fire* made what was probably the most important affirmation in the form of a pantomime ballet since *L'Après Midi d'un Faune, Le Sacre du Printemps* and *Til Eulenspiegel*. Hagar, the heroine of *Pillar of Fire,* goes to a brothel to escape respectable virginity. She is re-introduced to domestic life by a man who formerly showed preference for her younger sister.

The moral of this ballet seems to be that the physical nature of woman is stronger than society, an idea that has been insufficiently explored by many a contemporary commentator on the political scene and the course of international affairs.

Tudor left the Ballet Theatre company as choreographer and dancer in 1950 to become a director of the Ballet Theatre and of the Metropolitan Opera Ballet School. He taught at the Juilliard School and in 1963 was appointed artistic director of the Royal Swedish Ballet. Currently, he is artistic director of Lucia Chase's American Ballet Theatre.

No American works of importance were produced by Ballet Theatre in 1942-43. Agnes de Mille's *Three Virgins and a Devil* and *Black Ritual* were in the repertoire, but were of little consequence. Miss de Mille was to find her work understood and appreciated elsewhere. Her rustic, romping *Rodeo* was produced with sympathy and charm by Ballet Russe, and her first lyric composition, with Katharine Sergava in the leading role, evoked the true spirit of Lynn Riggs' *Green Grow the Lilacs* in the ballet that lifted *Oklahoma* out of the category of just another musical comedy.

In 1942, Michel Fokine died. Baranova later joined a Broadway musical, and Alicia Markova announced her intention of leaving Ballet Theatre to work for Billy Rose.

Agnes de Mille's *Tally-Ho,* produced by Ballet Theatre was, choreographically speaking, an unhappy blend of genuine rustic and false sophistication, although the music by Glück, the costumes and sets by Motley, and the miming of Anton Dolin and Janet Reed, a young American dancer trained by William Christensen, and the San Francisco Ballet, made up for some of the bad composition.

Antony Tudor's *Romeo and Juliet,* a suite of mimed tableaux from Shakespeare, was an elaborate spectacle done with more earnestness than felicity. The greatest of English poets speaks most eloquently to the heart and with less need of visual embellishment and interpretation than perhaps any other poet. *Romeo and Juliet* without the text was embarrassing, and sometimes as awkwardly indiscreet as Madam Malaprop.

The critics called it a dull season for Russian Ballet, always excepting the brilliant dancing of Markova in *Giselle,* and of Youskevitch and Danilova, stars of the Ballet Russe, who were acknowledged the greatest classic male dancer and the only "prima ballerina assoluta" since Mordkin and Pavlowa. A dull season for Russian Ballet and English Ballet choreographers, but not so for the American dance companies who had played in schools, in Young Men's and Young Women's Hebrew Associations, who had rehearsed when other dancers were resting from their performances in the Broadway theatres, who had studied in the summer and given shows to finance their dance education and to pay for a rehearsal pianist and the hire of their halls. These earnest and ardent and indomitable young American dancers who were ready to dance even though it meant half starving and freezing, saw in the triumph of Jerome Robbins' *Fancy Free,* produced by Ballet Theatre, the fulfillment of their dreams and struggles. Here, at last, was a real American ballet, rich with the great traditions of great dancing. The color and style of Russian dancing, the lyric restraint of English ballet—these Jerome Robbins had learned and made part of himself. But *Fancy Free* had more than these qualities; it had the pace of America and the droll swagger and wit of Americans who, whether soldier, sailor, tinker, tailor, rich man, poor man, beggarman or thief, enjoy a laugh at their own expense.

Fancy Free, to the music of Leonard Bernstein and the décor of Oliver Smith, danced by Jerome Robbins, Harold Laing, John Kriza, Janet Reed, Shirley Eckl, Muriel Bentley and Hugh Cooper, was the beginning of a new chapter in American Ballet. A coming of age, perhaps, with the help of the finest teachers from Russia, England, Continental Europe and America.

BIBLIOGRAPHY

Armitage, Merle. *Martha Graham*. Los Angeles: Lynton R. Kistler, 1937.

Balanchine, George. *Balanchine's Complete Story of the Great Ballets*. New York: Doubleday & Co., 1954.

Beaumont, Cyril. *Michel Fokine and His Ballets*. London: C. W. Beaumont, 1935.

————. *Vaslav Nijinsky*. London: C. W. Beaumont, 1932.

Bourman, Anatole, and Lyman, D. *The Tragedy of Nijinsky*. London, 1937.

Brahms, Caryl. *Footnotes to the Ballet*. London: Lovat-Dickson, 1936.

Chujoy, Anatole, and Manchester, P. W. *Dance Encyclopedia*. New York: Simon and Schuster, 1967.

Cohen, Selma Jeanne, ed. *The Modern Dance: Seven Statements of Belief*. Introduction by Selma Jeanne Cohen. Wesleyan University, 1965, 1966.

Denby, Edwin. *Looking at the Dance*. Pellegrini & Cudahy, 1949.

Desti, Mary. *The Untold Story of Isadora Duncan's Life, 1921–27*. New York: Liveright, 1929.

Divoire, Fernand. *Isadora Duncan, Fille de Promethée*. Illustrated by E. A. Bourdelle. Paris: Editions des Muses Françaises, 1919.

Dreier, Katherine S. *Shawn, the Dancer*. New York: A. S. Barnes & Co., Inc., 1933.

Duncan, Irma, and MacDougall, Allan Rose. *Isadora Duncan's Russian Days and Her Last Years in France*. New York, 1929.

Duncan, Isadora. *My Life*. New York: Liveright, 1928.

"Essays, Stories and Remarks about Merce Cunningham," *Dance Perspective*, No. 34 (Summer 1968).

Ewen, David. *Complete Book of the American Musical Theater*. New York: Holt, Rinehart & Winston, 1970.

Farnsworth, Marjorie. *The Ziegfeld Follies: A History in Text and Pictures*. New York: Crown, Bonanza Books, 1956.

Gautier, Theophile. *The Romantic Ballet*. Translated by Cyril Beaumont. London: C. W. Beaumont, 1932.

Genthe, Arnold. *Twenty-four Studies of Isadora Duncan*. New York: Mitchell Kennerley, 1929.

Gilbert, Douglas. *History of American Vaudeville*. New York: Dover, 1940.

Goldman, William. *The Season*. New York: Harcourt Brace Jovanovich, 1969.

Gruen, John. *The Private World of Ballet*. New York: Viking Press, 1974.

Haskell, Arnold, and Nouvel, Walter. *Diaghileff, His Artistic and Private Life*. New York: Simon & Schuster, 1935.

Hastings, Baird. "The Denishawn Era (1914–31)." *Dance Index*, Vol. 1, No. 6, June, 1942.

Kirstein, Lincoln. *Ballet Alphabet*. Illustrated by Paul Cadmus. New York, 1939.

_____. *Nijinsky Dancing*. Commentary by Lincoln Kirstein. New York: Alfred Knopf, 1975.

Klosty, James, ed. *Merce Cunningham*. New York: Saturday Review Press, 1975.

Lafitte, Jean-Paul. *Les Dances · d'Isadora Duncan*. Preface by Elie Faure. Paris: Mercure de France, 1910.

Laurie, Joe, Jr. *Vaudeville: From the Honky-Tonk to the Palace*. Port Washington, New York: Kennikat Press, 1972.

Lieven, Prince Peter. *The Birth of Ballets-Russes*. Boston: Houghton Mifflin Co., 1936.

Lifar, Serge. Serge Diaghileff, *His Life, His Work, His Legend*. London: Putnam.

Lloyd, Margaret. "Relation of Music to Movement." *Christian Science Monitor*, March 1932.

MacLean, Albert F., Jr. *American Vaudeville as Ritual*. University of Kentucky Press, 1965.

Martin, John. *Introduction to the Dance*. New York: W. W. Norton & Co., 1939.

_____. *The Modern Dance*. New York: A. S. Barnes & Co., Inc., 1933.

Maynard, Olga. *American Modern Dance*. Boston: Little Brown, 1965.

McDonagh, Don. *Martha Graham: A Biography*. New York: Praeger, 1973.

Montenegro, Robert. *Vaslav Nijinsky*. London: C. W. Beaumont, 1913.

Moritz, Charles, ed. *Current Biography*. Bronx, N.Y.: N.W. Wilson Co., 1964 (Paul Taylor), 1967 (Robert Joffrey), 1968 (Alvin Ailey), 1969 (Jerome Robbins).

Nijinsky, Romola. *Nijinsky*. London: V. Gollancz, 1933.

_____. (Editor). *The Diary of Nijinsky*. New York: Simon & Schuster, 1936.

The Notebooks of Martha Graham. Introduction by Nancy Wilson Ross. New York: Harcourt Brace Jovanovich, 1973.

Noverre, M. *Lettres sur la Danse et sur les Ballets*.

Oukrainsky, Serge. *My Two Years with Anna Pavlowa*. Los Angeles: I.M. Suttonhouse.

Percival, John. *Experimental Dance.* New York: Putnam, 1971.
_____. *Modern Ballet.* Studio Vista Ltd.-Blue Star House, 1970.
Propert, W. A. *The Russian Ballet in Western Europe, 1909–20.* London: John Lane the Bodley Head, Ltd., 1921.
Saint Georges, H. de, and Gautier, Theophile. "Giselle, ou Les Wilis." Paris: Beautés de L'Opéra, 1845.
Sargeant, Winthrop. "Biography of Martha Graham." *The Dance Observer,* May, 1934–37.
Selden, Elizabeth. *The Dancer's Quest.* University of California Press, 1935.
Shawn, Ted. *American Ballet.* Introduction by Havelock Ellis. New York: Henry Holt & Co., 1926.
_____. *Gods Who Dance.* New York: E. P. Dutton & Co., 1929.
_____. *Ruth St. Denis, Pioneer and Prophet.* San Francisco: John Howell, 1920.
Sorell, Walter, ed. *The Dance Has Many Faces.* New York: Columbia University Press, 1966.
Stebbins, Genevieve. *Delsarte, System of Expression.* New York: Edgar Werner Publishing and Supply Co., 1902.
Stokes, Lewell. *Isadora Duncan, An Intimate Portrait.* London: Brentano, 1928.
Terry, Walter. *The Dance in America.* New York: Harper & Row, 1971.
Van Vechten, Carl. *Interpreters and Interpretations.* New York: Alfred Knopf, 1917.
"Vaslav Nijinsky." *Dance Index,* New York, 1942.
Whitworth, Geoffrey. *The Art of Nijinsky.* Illustrated by D. Mullock. New York: McBride, Nast & Co., 1913.
Young, Stark. "Martha Graham." *New Republic,* December 14, 1932.

Acknowledgement is also made to the Performing Arts Research Center and the Dance Collection, New York Public Library at Lincoln Center, Astor, Lenox and Tilden Foundations.

INDEX

233

BARTON COLLEGE LIBRARY

3 6500 00253 5125

792.809   83-0828
P182t
Palmer
Theatrical dancing in
America.

Atlantic Christian College Library
Wilson, N. C.

P182t